Mozart
BLOOMS IN
WOODSTOCK
THE ILLINOIS FESTIVAL THAT COULD!

Mozart
BLOOMS IN
WOODSTOCK
THE ILLINOIS FESTIVAL THAT COULD!

WOODSTOCK *Mozart* Festival

ANITA WHALEN

To all those who devoted their efforts
to this endeavor

Contents

Introduction   ix

Chapter 1   **PRELUDE**   1

Chapter 2   **OVERTURE**   25

Chapter 3   **SERENADE**   41

Chapter 4   **CONCERTO**   57

Chapter 5   **SYMPHONY**   73

Chapter 6   **INTERLUDE**   89

Chapter 7   **FINALE**   105

Postlude   127

Anecdotes   133

About the Author   139

Index   141

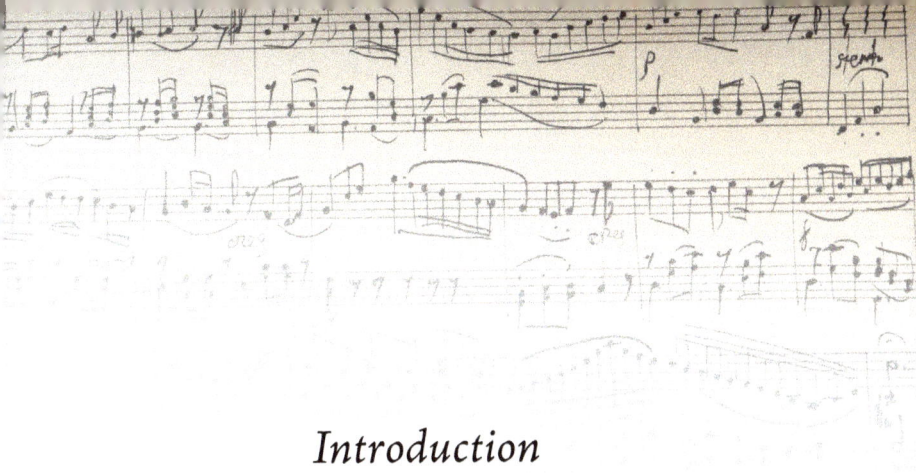

Introduction

During the summer of 2018, I received a phone call from Hinsdale, Illinois, resident Jake Dickens. He mentioned that he was a member of a board of directors planning a new Schubert Festival in Oak Park, Illinois, to be held at Frank Lloyd Wright's Unity Temple. The group had already held two festivals, one of which was a piano recital by Ralph Votapek. Future annual festivals were to feature four concerts: song and piano recitals as well as chamber music concerts performed by members of the Chicago Symphony and Chicago's Lyric Opera orchestras.

Jake mentioned that he and his fellow board members had been so impressed by the Woodstock Mozart Festival's performances (in Woodstock, Illinois) over the years, they hoped that as the festival's former director, I could shed some light on how they could successfully launch their new project.

In the early fall, Jake invited me to have lunch with the board and the artistic director, Martha Swisher, called Marty. We had a lively exchange, but I did not feel I helped them much without access to information on my computer and other materials. So I suggested that Marty come to my home office where I could quickly look up information and hopefully better answer their questions.

Marty, along with Jake's wife, Belinda Bremner, came to my office and asked several questions. I answered them as best I could; however, the fact that the two venues and communities were quite different made an equitable comparison difficult. Nonetheless, after a few hours, the ladies were ready to leave. On their way out, Belinda said, "You *are* going to write a book about this!" to which I answered, "Oh I don't think so . . . it is in the past."

However, when my old computer crashed during the summer of 2019, I took the opportunity to upgrade to a Mac. After computer guru Mike Potter of ESC! Technologies Group set up my new Mac and transferred all my files to it, I thought, "Well, now that I have this new computer, what should I do with it?" In a rather flippant manner I said, "Maybe now I will write my book about the festival," to which Mike answered, "You SHOULD!" I added, "And you will be my editor," to which he answered, "You just need to start."

Sometime in the late fall of 2019, I decided to just "start" as Mike had suggested. Because the events of my childhood had such a strong and lasting influence on my relationship with music, I decided to start at the beginning . . . when I was born, in 1942. Within an hour or two, I had finished the first section of the first chapter and put it on the kitchen table to see if my husband, Charlie, might be interested in looking at it. I thought, "If he thinks it isn't worth my time and effort, I will not continue."

Not long after, he did read it and said, "This is really entertaining. I am interested to hear what happens next!" And that is how this book began.

Chapter 1

PRELUDE

Where to begin? I suppose on July 20, 1942.
I was born at the New York Hospital on this date and named Anita Louise Schlier. My mother and I were in the maternity ward where everyone could see the troop ships departing on the East River for Europe. On the day we arrived home at my grandmother's home in Flushing, New York, a recording of *Orpheus in the Underworld* by Offenbach (famous for its Parisian Can Can music) was blaring for all the neighbors to hear through open windows in celebration of my arrival. By then my father had begun what later became an extensive classical music record collection. At the time, the three of us lived with my grandmother and her second husband in the Flushing neighborhood of the borough of Queens, on Long Island.

When I was two and a half, we traveled cross-country on a troop train to the Los Angeles area, where my father's company (U.S. Rubber Company, now Uniroyal) manufactured synthetic rubber on behalf of the war effort. We lived in a small two-bedroom home in Gardena, California, and

I distinctly remember many outings to Knott's Berry Farm, the Hollywood Bowl for concerts, and to "free" afternoon concerts with dance opportunities in the park, compliments of Xavier Cugat and his Latin band. Since my parents were avid ballroom dancers, I remember the three of us dancing—them as a couple and me alone. I loved the over-the-top infectious music . . . who wouldn't?

I also remember the layout of our apartment and hearing music from my father's record collection. My favorite classical recording was of ballet music, at least that is what I thought. The recording, *Les Sylphides*, was of orchestrated piano works by Chopin that had been arranged into a medley for a ballet of the same name by Russian choreographer Michael Fokine. I remember dancing around the living room to *Les Sylphides* and deciding at age three that Chopin was my favorite composer.

Knowing the music was by Chopin stems from the fact that my parents (knowledgeable fans of classical music), often discussed composers and their works as well as artists and conductors with whom they had become familiar in New York. My mother had encountered many renowned artists and entertainers while working at A. Sulka and Company (a high-end men's haberdashery on Fifth Avenue) before marrying my father. Over the years she spoke about her clients, Jascha Heifetz, Leopold Stokowski, and others who became household names.

Clearly, music was the most important interest in my parents' lives. I attribute this to their cultural heritage, as both were born in Hungary before coming to the United States with their parents as children.

My mother was very talented in acting and dancing and was active in the Hungarian Little Theatre in New York. My father studied violin during his childhood and even through his college years as a night school student of accounting at NYU while working full time for the U.S. Rubber Company during the day. In addition, he had a beautiful tenor voice and loved to sing.

After the war ended, we left California and lived in St. Albans, West Virginia, for a year while my father shut down a plant no longer necessary for the war effort. He was then transferred to Naugatuck, Connecticut, where he continued in the chemical division of his company. Since housing was scarce after the war, my parents decided I should live with my grandmother in her home in Flushing. In the meantime, they lived in a rooming house in Naugatuck until suitable housing arrangements became available for the three of us. However, they drove every Friday evening to visit us in Flushing for the weekend.

The experience of living with my grandmother in New York was one of the richest in my life. As a European, she cooked and baked almost everything from scratch: bread, strudel, noodles, doughnuts, and many wonderful Hungarian specialties . . . with my help of course . . . at age six. The change from going to school in West Virginia for the first half of first grade to the New York City public school system for the second half of first grade was unnerving, to say the least. I vividly remember one experience that, in the end, has to do with immigration, now such an important topic in our country.

My grandmother had many Hungarian friends with whom she visited and spoke to in her native language. One day, I just did not want to go to the big, scary school after crossing the big, scary Long Island Expressway with all those fast cars zooming by, even though my grandmother held my hand and safely crossed with me.* Thinking my grandmother did not know much about American ways, I announced that there was no school on this particular day. My grandmother wanted to know the reason; I said the teacher told us it was a vacation day. My grandparents began discussing in English what holiday it might be: Washington's birthday, Columbus Day, etc. I listened to the list of possibilities, my eyes getting bigger and bigger as I wondered how they knew all this "American stuff." Finally, my grandmother said she was going to call the teacher. At this I blurted out, "Oh NO, don't do that!," giving myself away. Out came my jacket, and off we went to school. Obviously, at this stage of my life, I was not familiar with the naturalization for citizenship process which my grandparents had obviously undergone.

Otherwise, I enjoyed weekly cultural outings with my grandmother that I will never forget: seeing Renoir's paintings at the Metropolitan Museum of Art, which made a dramatic life-long impression; viewing the giant whale and amazing animal scenes at the Museum of Natural History; seeing the Rockettes dance to Ravel's "Bolero" at Radio City Music Hall. The only problem with this experience was that I remember thinking the music was rather boring . . . the same tune over and over . . .

As I mentioned, my parents came to visit every weekend, always an exciting time for me.

---

* In 1948, what is now the Long Island Expressway was called Horace Harding Boulevard. Traffic lights enabled pedestrians to cross the boulevard. However, I don't remember a light at the intersection we needed to cross, making it seem dangerous. There were also bus stops. Today, the volume of traffic and speeds on the LIE have increased tremendously. I noticed while in the area some years ago that pedestrian crossing bridges have been constructed, there are no longer traffic lights and, I assume, no bus stops.

We swam at Jones Beach, shopped in Manhattan, and visited with friends. Another weekend activity was tuning into the Met broadcasts on Saturdays at noon. This became a ritual in our family. My dad and I sat together, he on a straight-backed chair (this being serious), and I on an ottoman next to him as he told the story of what was happening in the opera. I vividly remember how moved I was when we were listening to *La Bohème.* During Act IV, the opera's lead, Mimi, is dying of consumption and her friend Colline, in a touching aria, bids farewell to his overcoat, which he is going to sell for money to engage a doctor. At this I began to cry, and then my father started crying. I soon came to understand that crying while listening to music is a popular Hungarian pastime.

While living with my grandmother, I enjoyed my own favorite pastimes: cooking with her in the kitchen, reading my first-grade textbooks to her while she ironed, and picking out tunes on the old upright piano in the recreation room in her basement.

Although no one in the family had played the piano, friends had asked my grandmother to store their upright piano temporarily for them while the house was being built. She agreed, and the piano was lowered into the basement before the descending concrete steps were added. Some may remember the trap doors that folded over these entrances. Once the concrete steps were added, there was no way to get the piano out. Luckily for me, I enjoyed picking out tunes, eventually playing with two hands, that is, with simple harmony in the left hand. My greatest frustration was with the "Blue Danube Waltz" as maneuvering the required jumps in chords with the left hand accurately was difficult. To my consternation, I never completely succeeded at this.

By the end of the school year, I was able to move to Connecticut and live with my parents, who had found a nice house. I loved being in a neighborhood with friends, which was not the case while living with my grandmother. There were no other young children in her neighborhood. I began the second grade in the large schoolhouse located on one side of the village square. This, in itself, confirmed Naugatuck to be a charming traditional New England town with a beautiful Congregational church on another side of the square. I remember a wonderful concert of Leroy Anderson's delightful, scintillating music conducted by the composer himself in that square.

There was an old upright piano right at the front of the class-room, and the music teacher visited us once a week to lead us in singing. This was hands down my favorite activity at school. One day, before we began, it came to the teacher's attention that one of the students' birthdays was on that day. He asked if anyone in the class could play "Happy Birthday" on the piano. I raised my hand, moved to the bench, and knocked out "Happy Birthday" while everyone sang. Then I sat down and never gave it another thought. Looking back on this experience of playing in public at age seven in a totally relaxed, nonchalant state, was something I often wished I could recreate later in life upon demand.

The same music teacher was also the choral director of the community men's chorus, which my father had joined. With his beautiful tenor voice and knowledge of music, he was a welcome addition. At the men's choral rehearsal following my "Happy Birthday" "performance," the director approached him and mentioned that he didn't know his daughter played the piano.

My dad said, "What? I don't think so. You must have her confused with someone else." To this, the director insisted that, indeed, it was I who had played "Happy Birthday" for the class, and that if I was not taking piano lessons, my parents should definitely have me begin. It is important to note that during my parents' weekend visits, we were so busy I never ventured downstairs to the piano.

Since we did not have a piano in Connecticut, we went into New York to pick one out. In a large warehouse setting, we decided on a new console Baldwin Acrosonic, and a teacher was engaged. She was preparing her Carnegie Hall debut recital. I am not surprised that she was quite lenient with me, as I later learned by becoming a teacher myself. There is a lot to teaching, which I do not think had been her focus. But it was a very positive experience for me. I could tell she loved teaching me because I caught on fast. Learning piano seemed very easy. "What's there to it . . . just enjoy!"

My bubble soon burst when my grandmother asked a Hungarian family friend to her house to check on how I was doing when we visited. I do not remember the man's name, but I knew he was important by his serious demeanor. Most assuredly schooled at the Franz Liszt Academy in Budapest, he was heavily engaged as an orchestral arranger for Broadway productions. I had my John Thompson's *Teaching Little Fingers to Play* book, in which I thought I had mastered every piece. Well, let me tell you, this man was a royal pain in the neck with all his corrections! It was a dramatic introduction to what my future with the piano was to become.

It is worth noting that at about the time I began piano lessons, my mother also enrolled me in a beginning ballet class. The dance master came to Naugatuck twice a week from New York and put the class through the paces. I had always wanted to be a ballerina—such a romantic art—and of course, all ballerinas were beautiful. Again, I was in for a rude awakening.

The dance master was a real professional who barked orders and constantly was *on* every student—bending, pulling, repositioning into what were the most contortionistic and painful positions we had to persist in during our workouts.

This was not what I thought ballet was about. I also noticed that I was not one of the best in the class. There was one girl who was very adept and pliable. For her, it all seemed "natural." After three months my mother discontinued the dance classes (much to my relief) with the following expression: "You will never be a dancer, but you might be a decent piano player."

My father was transferred again in 1951, this time to Baton Rouge, Louisiana, to open a new chemical plant for his company. My mother immediately tracked down a piano teacher, whom I came to understand was the most highly regarded in the community.

The teacher tested my skills and informed my mother that I was not reading music so she would not take me as a student. Apparently, I had been playing by ear. After hearing my former teacher play, I had been able to duplicate those tunes. My mother was mortified but asked what could be done.

The teacher had a studio with two other young teachers whom she had trained to teach beginners. I was handed over to one of them, who apparently did the job. Soon, she took me as a student.

We lived in Baton Rouge for seven years, what I would call my formative years. I seemed to do well with my piano study. I gave a recital at home when I was eleven and was included in a piano quartet during my years in junior high.* My partner at one of the two pianos was a friend. After preparing our parts, two other students joined us to practice at the two pianos in our teacher's studio. We gave a recital at the Baton Rouge Women's Club and had an appearance on local television. My aunt, who was living in southern Louisiana, reported that their family and friends had seen our performance on TV. We had become "famous"!

My piano partner's parents were also from New York, and they were friends with my parents. Both sets of parents were strong supporters of the Baton Rouge Symphony, and many famous artists soloed with the orchestra: Artur Rubinstein and others, including Claudio Arrau.

After Mr. Arrau's performance, my partner and I met him in the Green Room and received his autograph. During this time, the piano on which he had performed was pushed off the stage into the wings. While going that way to leave the hall we stopped to play one of our encore duets, "Windy City Boogie," on the concert grand. Mr. Arrau happened to walk that way after we began. He stopped, listened through our performance, and warmly congratulated and encouraged us. Coincidentally, both my piano partner and I have lived our adult lives in or near the "Windy City," where we became instrumental in the Chicago area's music scene.**

It is important to mention the experiences I had while growing up listening to music with my parents. As you can imagine, they had heard many artists at the Met and at orchestral and other concerts in New York, and thereby had developed their

---

* A piano quartet involves two pianos and four players, with two players at each piano.
** My partner in the piano quartet was Helen Herzog, now Helen Zell, former chair of the Chicago Symphony Orchestra, and currently vice chair.

own definitive tastes and opinions for standards of performance. I have since come to define their listening skills not only as discerning, but also as highly discriminating. Webster's actual definition: "The discrimination that develops through listening to a lot of great music." The experiences I had during many years of attending concerts with them and hearing their remarks is clearly what shaped my own listening skills, tastes, and performance standards. By now I have come to view these as the most critically influential for my future in music.

A prophetic experience occurred when my parents befriended the orchestra's music director, Russian conductor Emil Cooper. He often came to our house for dinner, where he and my parents discussed the New York music scene, including artists and conductors whom my mother had even known personally. In addition, Maestro Cooper loved my mother's Hungarian cooking. When he came over, it was never boring.

He had a vibrant, outrageous personality which, with my mother's animated disposition, produced an atmosphere I can only describe as entertaining "fireworks"! They joked and kibitzed about the music industry, and I listened and learned a lot, never imagining that what I heard on these occasions would have anything to do with my future.

It was not until many years later when I read Igor Stravinsky's autobiography that I learned Maestro Cooper had premiered many of his works in London, Paris, and at the Mariinsky Theatre in St. Petersburg, Russia, where he had been music director of the orchestra. I never had any idea of the gift of exposure I was receiving about the orchestra world so early in my life until much later . . . something I have come to call the "Stravinsky Connection."

My entry into high school marked the end of the piano quartet (described in the previous section) when my partner's father was transferred back to New York. I continued with my piano study, only to move again, just before my junior year, to Joliet, Illinois, where my father's company ran the Joliet Arsenal. The year was 1958.

My mother again tracked down the most respected piano teacher. She happened to be a faculty member at Roosevelt University in Chicago, and she came out to Joliet two days a week to teach at the local conservatory. Her name was Blythe Owen, and she immediately took me under her wing, opening the door to many opportunities. The first was to connect me to the high school orchestra, then led by Peter Labella, a most encouraging and endearing director and teacher.

Because the Great Joliet Township High School, as I have come to call it, had an enrollment of four thousand, and because the arts were more important than sports there at the time, other serious music students were in the orchestra. But because many orchestral works do not include piano scores, those of us who were piano players became the librarians, accompanists, and chamber musicians. Again, I am amazed at how much this would prepare me for what later became a career in orchestra management.

I distinctly remember feeling thrilled at a rehearsal before a performance at another high school, to which we had been invited to play. I even remember the work, Ralph Vaughan Williams's *English Folksong Suite's* "March: Seventeen Come Sunday." With this jaunty introduction to the concert, I felt I had died and gone to heaven—being involved in the sounds and experiences as well as enjoying the camaraderie of those whose love of music matched mine.

At the end of my senior year, I played the first movement of the Grieg Piano Concerto with the orchestra. By then I had decided, with the encouragement of my teacher and Mr. Labella, to pursue a career in music. With my pursuit of heavier repertoire, my Acrosonic piano was not holding up very well. At the time I was practicing for Chicago area competitions, accompanying, playing chamber music, and practicing the Grieg concerto. My parents and grandmother decided I needed a grand piano, and so began the search with trips to the Lyon & Healy store in Chicago. Eventually, I liked one instrument above the rest available on the floor, and a Steinway L (Living Room Grand) was purchased.

I would like to mention that during this time, my parents subscribed to the Chicago Symphony, where Fritz Reiner was the music director. Although the Baton Rouge Symphony was quite good for a regional orchestra, the elevated standard of performances I heard while attending concerts of the Chicago Symphony was a revelation. I soon became aware of the magnified dramatic impact and more deeply moving inspirational effects of live music while in the presence of this great orchestra. Also, by now my father had acquired an extensive record library of works performed by many great orchestras, conductors, and artists of the time, which I heard over and over.

Soon I auditioned for the music school of which both of my mentors were alumni, the Eastman School of Music in Rochester, New York. I passed the audition with the suggestion that I acquire a stronger background in music theory before entering in the fall.

Because I had attended summer music camp at the University at Illinois (U of I) on a scholarship the summer before, I contacted the piano faculty member with whom I had studied,

Dr. William Schoonmaker, about this request from Eastman, thinking I would go to summer school at the U of I to better prepare myself in theory. He suggested that I come to Champaign, Illinois, to audition for a scholarship, which I thought meant for the summer class, so I did. Lo and behold, I was offered a scholarship to attend the U of I Music School for my entire future undergraduate education as an applied piano major! I was flabbergasted, and knowing how much money would be saved, I accepted the offer and became a student of Soulima Stravinsky, the son of Igor Stravinsky. And so, the "Stravinsky Connection" continued.

By the end of my junior year at the U of I, I realized I did not want a career in "applied piano" (now called "piano performance" at many schools). I understood that I was not equipped in many ways for this kind of career, beginning with my childhood experience of knowing what real professional performers were like—with their fantastic technique, ability to quickly learn and memorize massive and extremely difficult works, and temperaments that enabled them to not feel intimidated when playing in public. These were qualities I did not possess, and at that point I also did not think I would ever teach piano, since I was also interested in other subjects which were impossible to explore because the required curriculum in music concentrates mainly on music. So I transferred into the College of Liberal Arts and Sciences.

I have always been interested in how people think and act as individuals and in groups, so I signed up for psychology and sociology courses. I also loved literature and added several of those courses to my curriculum while expanding my horizons with the additional liberal arts requirements and other options. With student leadership opportunities, as president of my sorority and secretary of the campus Panhellenic Council, I became interested in organizational government. I continued at the university for two more years and graduated with a degree in psychology.

Just before graduation, I met my husband, Charlie, who was teaching agricultural law and traveling the state through the University's Extension Service to advise farmers on legal matters. Of those I had dated outside of music school, he was the only one who listened to classical music. I was hooked . . . not only by this, of course, but also by his many other wonderful attributes. We were married in May 1966 and left immediately for Offutt Air Force Base outside of Omaha, Nebraska, where he served in the legal office until 1969. Because of the Vietnam War, all eligible young men were subject to the draft during this time, which was an incentive for Charlie to enlist for officer's training to be in the Judge Advocate General Corps so he could continue in his field.

I had worked in the personnel department of the accounting firm of Arthur Andersen in Chicago for a short time after graduation, and I looked for a job in that field in Omaha. However, no one was hiring military wives due to the precarious nature of their tenure in the area. If their husbands were sent to Vietnam, as many were, the wives invariably returned to their hometowns.

Instead, I unexpectedly inherited a class of thirty piano students from the wife of an Air Force colonel who was transferring to another base. I had never met this person, but she had heard about me through the military wives' grapevine. My parents shipped my Steinway piano out to Omaha, and I took on the thirty students, not having a clue as to how to begin teaching them properly. I made many trips to the Omaha music store and did my best, which I am afraid was not very good.

At the end of my first year as a teacher all my students were presented in recital. I knew there was a German couple by the name of Baer who taught piano in the town of Bellevue near the base. They were looking for someone to assist them with their growing class and apparently had heard about me. I saw Mrs. Baer come into the recital and walk out at the end, never saying a word to me. I got the message.

By the time Charlie's three-year military tenure ended in 1969, we had two children: a daughter, Julia, and son, Charles, whom we call Chuck. We moved to suburban Naperville, Illinois, and Charlie joined a Chicago law firm. I very much wanted to continue working, and despite not having intended to teach piano, that is what I ended up doing. Since we had two babies, going to an office each day was not an option.

An outstanding pianist and pedagogue, Elvina Pearce, happened to live in Naperville. She had had a career at the New School for Music Study (a piano teaching research institution) in Princeton, New Jersey, before marrying the local high school choral director, John Pearce. Both had outstanding reputations, for good reason, as they were exceptional in their fields. Luckily, I was able to consult with Elvina on how to become a competent piano teacher and soon developed a large class of students. Eventually I joined an outgrowth of the New School, the piano teaching research company called National Keyboard Arts, and became one of its consultants and workshop technicians.

With the Keyboard Arts association came another wonderful opportunity, to coach piano works with the organization's composer, David Kraehenbuehl. With undergraduate degrees in piano and mathematics from the University of Illinois, David became the protégé of Paul Hindemith while studying for a master's degree in composition at Yale. When Hindemith returned to Germany after World War II, he recommended that David take his place as head of the theory and composition department, which he did for some years. However, David's talents were recognized in other places, and eventually he left Yale to pursue other interests and opportunities. One of these was in piano teaching at the New School and then as cofounder of National Keyboard Arts.

Because David visited Chicago every few months on business, I took the opportunity to prepare piano works for his visits in order to expand my own repertoire and learn from him. An unusually rich and rewarding pursuit ensued: that is, to study works not only with a pianist, but a pianist who was also a composer. David's brilliance was recognized by all who knew him, and to learn via a composer's perspective was indeed a unique and valuable opportunity.

Around this time, I also opened a music school in downtown Naperville and eventually became Certification Chairman of the Illinois State Music Teachers Association.

There are many teachers like me who did not have degrees in music; in fact, many have no conservatory experience at all, but still purport to being piano teachers because they can, to some degree, play the piano. It is also known in the teaching industry that having a degree in music is no guarantee of competency for teaching. So the national and state music teachers associations developed teaching certification programs by which those with and without degrees can obtain professional teaching credentials.

The Illinois State Music Teachers certification program needed to be revised to be more rigorous. When I was assigned chairman, I invited two highly regarded certified piano teachers to join me. One was very good with younger children, the other with those more advanced. I sort of fit in the middle.

We revamped the program, which I handled in what I suppose was a rather businesslike way with memos, reports, etc. I had always been fascinated by business, my father having been a corporate executive who had attended the High School of Commerce in New York before going to NYU. I watched him type one hundred words a minute without errors on a manual typewriter, create excellent business letters, and even write shorthand, which I never learned to do. (I still cannot type one hundred words a minute perfectly on a computer keyboard with non-resistant keys!)

In any case, the teacher who was excellent with younger students was Dolores Piccirilli. The teacher of advanced students was Sally Bauer. She was married to conductor Harold Bauer, the music director of two suburban orchestras: New Philharmonic, at the College of DuPage in Glen Ellyn, Illinois, and the Fox River Valley Symphony in nearby Aurora, Illinois.

Sally told me at lunch one day that Harold had asked her to ask me if I would be interested in arts management. I am sure I looked bewildered when I answered, "You mean like Rudolph Bing?" As many probably remember, Rudolph Bing was the notorious, supposedly tyrannical, director of the Metropolitan Opera. He was the only person I knew of in that kind of work, so I said, "no," adding that I was not that type of person.

Sally pointed out that not all arts administrators needed to be like Rudolph Bing. Occasionally, we spoke about the possibility, but I never went to observe what an arts administrator does, as Sally suggested I do, by visiting the office of the Fox River Valley Symphony. I did not think much about it until I got a call from the president of the board asking if I would come in for an interview. He explained that the current manager was retiring with her husband to their vacation home in Wisconsin, and that the conductor, Harold Bauer, had suggested he call me.

To say I was surprised is an understatement. I told the president I had never done that kind of work. He said I should come to the interview anyway to see what it was about. I remember having a smart looking Albert Nippon business dress that would be appropriate. So I went, as I thought to myself, "on a lark."

I do not remember the questions posed to me, nor any that I asked, but two days later the president called to offer me the job. I was shocked and said, "But I've never done this before!" . . . to which he answered, "We think you'd be good at it." Perplexed, I told my family. Typical of college-age students, my kids suggested that the board probably couldn't get anyone else. In fact, I later learned that others who had worked in the field had indeed applied and been interviewed for the position.

Here I was, starting all over again to do something I knew nothing about. Interestingly, I had already signed up for a month-long music and art study tour in Hungary. After I got there and heard and saw the standard, I thought it was like going to the Mecca of classical music performances. The experience, in a country where music is so important, was fabulous. I soon learned that there, not all conductors are called Maestro, but are considered to be doing a regular job like other professionals: accountants, lawyers, managers, and so on.

I also noticed that there was plenty of room in the concert hall seats for people to be comfortable, plenty of leg room so as not to feel confined. While watching the orchestras, I was impressed with how each section leaned into every phrase together as one, anticipating what they were to play. I was most impressed with the number of children of grade school age at all concerts with their parents, attentive and engaged, just as I had been. This was in 1988, before the Berlin Wall came down. The one thing that was deeply disturbing, however, was the sadness of the people; they walked down the street looking at the pavement, seldom up. By contrast, my parents and extended family members who had emigrated to America were spirited and upbeat, not having gone through the devastation of World War II and the subsequent Russian occupation.

When I returned from Hungary, I almost immediately went into a week-long, intense training program offered by the then American Symphony Orchestra League, subsequently renamed the League of American Orchestras. Because the program was held in a hotel in Chicago and was a day-and-night marathon, I stayed at the hotel. I loved it! The intensity, professionalism, rapid pace, and of course, the concerts. I hung out with trainees like myself, but also with experienced administrators, conductors from other countries . . . the pros. It was intoxicating!

When the first session of the training course began, we were asked to stand and tell our backgrounds. I said I had studied applied piano and also had a degree in psychology. The session leader replied that this was the "magic combination for arts management." Really? I'd thought I'd been a failure for not having finished my music degree. What a surprise! Maybe I did belong somewhere after all. And in fact, that's exactly how I felt. I had found my place and a career that seemed to fit.

I was with the Fox River Valley Symphony for four years. What was supposed to be a part-time job at very part-time pay turned out to be a full-time job and more effort at very part-time pay. It was all new, and not easy, but there were many who helped me along the way. An important person was a woman who had befriended my former colleague, the conductor's wife, Sally Bauer. She was an accountant, whose husband had been transferred by his company to an operation here, and she pitched in by creating financial procedures for the Symphony. I was involved every step of the way, an enormous blessing because that was the one area lacking in my background.

I also knew, from my experience at home growing up, how important a volunteer association was. Unfortunately, the orchestra did not have one. There was a small group of interested women from the area who sold cookies and punch at intermissions of the concerts at nearby Fermi Lab to earn money for the orchestra's Young Artists Competition, but that was all.

With the assistance of League of American Orchestras' legendary Volunteer Association expert Audrey Baird, we expanded the group to include women from Naperville and other areas. This energetic new group's first initiative was a beautiful and effective introductory event featuring the entertaining and unique Audrey Baird herself. Audrey was an expert at converting nonbelievers, not only to become believers, but also to become joiners and doers, in this case to join and do for the new Symphony Foxes. Remember Ethyl Merman? That was Audrey—with a more modulated voice and her own little song and soft-shoe routine. They were charming, but most important, convincing.

The event was held in the expansive lobby of the new architecturally significant aquamarine glass office building on the nearby corporate corridor of Highway I-88. Also featured during the evening was a riveting performance of Claude Bolling's *Piano Jazz Suite*. Elaborate and lucrative Symphony Balls were held during the following two years, with strolling Viennese Strings, great dance bands, and fabulous raffle prizes. All three events were beautiful, glamorous, and very successful.

The orchestra had just gone through a transformational change, from a community orchestra of nonprofessionals to one of professionals. All potential players were auditioned by the conductor, including the new "professionals" and amateurs from the former community orchestra who wanted to continue to play and now be paid a modest sum. Of course, this did not sit well with those who were not professionals and who had been involved as players for many years. Many chose not to audition.

There were three byproducts of the new orchestral arrangement. One was that the audience of those who came to see and hear their neighbors and relatives on stage as community concert players no longer attended the concerts. So we began a series of "Prelude Parties" in supporters' homes to woo new attendees and subscribers with programs of chamber music, desserts, and pitches. Also, the venue had been moved from a high school auditorium to the recently restored and magnificent Paramount Theatre. As previously mentioned, the newly configured orchestra was to be paid, which meant that it now had increased expenses.

Although the Paramount was clearly a more desirable venue, and not that costly to rent, its restoration had absorbed a major portion of the fundraising capital available in the community. The orchestra, not as popular a draw, was in its shadow. I believe that during my training through the League I had learned that only 2 percent of the population was interested in classical music. So, by the time the orchestra became more expensive to maintain as a professional orchestra, even those who were well-to-do fans of classical music in the community had already invested generously in the Paramount.

We had a $15,000 deficit, and no matter what I did by initiating a new volunteer association that made money, and dedicating my own extraordinary effort, I could not reduce the deficit.

I called the League of American Orchestras' office in Washington, DC, and the notorious Ralph Black (the "Dean" as many called him) answered the phone. He told me to write a grant and get him "out there," which I did. When I picked him up at the Midway Airport in February, I knew he was not well, certainly not as I had seen him at the previous summer's League Conference. His pallor was gray and his walk seemed labored. Since my mother had had a heart attack with similar effects, I made sure throughout his visit that I had chairs available nearby, dropping him off and picking him up at entrances, and so on.

At a dinner with the board of directors and all the supporters I could gather, Ralph gave the most entertaining and stimulating pitch you can imagine. He talked to the board of directors the next day and had me call the *Naperville Sun* for a photo op and story.

The photographer and reporter came to my home and asked many questions. Then came the photo opportunity. Ralph told me to raise the lid on my grand piano and put some music on the lowered stand. Seating me on the bench, he stood over me, pointing to the open score as if he was explaining something on it. Ralph, who did not read a note of music!

Anita Whalen and Ralph Black

On his way back to the airport, he told me the group was looking to me for leadership and that he would return in May to help me plan. In the meantime, I was to do what he proceeded to suggest. When I dropped him off at the airport, I thanked him and said I would do my best. Two weeks later, I heard the news that Ralph had died of a heart attack. All of us who knew and leaned on him were devastated.

Ralph's photo with me at the piano is the last one taken of him. I not only have a copy of it on the wall of my studio, but also one on my desk.

In Ralph's place, the League sent out another consultant, Bill Weinrod. He was excellent; he saw clearly what needed to be done and made suggestions to the board of directors. On our way to the airport after his visit he said to me, "If the board does not go for what I suggested, you leave, and we'll help you get a job."

In essence, that is what happened, except that I did not turn to the League to help me get another job. Instead, I went back to school for a Certificate of Business Administration for running not-for-profits at my alma mater's Chicago campus, UIC, so that my credentials would be complete for the next job search.

Chapter 2

OVERTURE

During the time I was studying for the Certificate of Business Administration, I applied for a few positions with the Chicago Symphony. I was interviewed by the orchestra's president, Henry Fogel. I do not remember what the position was for the first interview, but I do remember his asking about the extent of my knowledge of the symphonic repertoire. Having no clue as to how to answer, I said that it was probably not as extensive as his, which I knew was correct. In hindsight, I am also sure that my own background was not too shabby, considering all the exposure I'd had over the years via my father's extensive record collection and the many concerts our family had attended. In any case, I was not called back for another interview for that job.

However, I was later interviewed again, this time by Mr. Fogel for the orchestra's education director job. With my teaching background and four years of orchestra management experience, I thought it would be a fit. But once again, I was not called back, and someone else got the job.

In February 1992, about a month before graduating from the business administration course at UIC, I received a late afternoon phone call from the president of the board of the Woodstock Mozart Festival in Woodstock, Illinois. I had heard of this festival and was aware of recent negative publicity it had received in the *Chicago Tribune*. There was a substantial deficit from the 1991 season, and the executive director, who was also the managing director of the Woodstock Opera House, had been dismissed from both positions.

By the time I received the phone call, the former director had left the area. She was, in fact, the wife of the festival's music director. He was also the music director of the Rockford Symphony for some years, but his contract with that organization had not been renewed. However, he had stayed behind and was planning to conduct the Mozart Festival during the coming summer season.

The president of the Mozart Festival seemed a bit frantic on the phone because the person who had agreed to take the position to execute the 1992 season had suddenly backed out. Anyone familiar with the effort required for staging a summer concert series knows how critical the time issue is by February.

Apparently, I had been recommended for the position by two orchestra administrators in the Chicago area. I later understood their description of me to have been: "If anyone can do a one-man band job, Anita Whalen can." That was exactly the reputation my father had after closing and opening plants after the war.

Knowing the Illinois Arts Council Grant was due in March, I offered to drive up to Woodstock for that evening's board meeting. I said I would write the grant to ensure the organization would not lose out on that important funding opportunity.

I fully intended to do this gratis and added that I would do it whether or not the board became interested in me, or I became interested in the position.

An additional concern for me about the festival, beside the unsavory publicity in the newspaper, was that the programming had been exclusively Mozart. Personally, I preferred variety programming, so I'd never considered venturing up to Woodstock to hear a performance.

At the board meeting, I handed over copies of my résumé. In the course of the evening, I heard how wonderful the Mozart Festival was and how much "people love it." I also saw the financial statement, which indicated the organization's deficit to be $15,000, the same amount I had just left at the Fox River Valley Symphony.

By the end of the meeting, I knew the board was determined to proceed with the sixth season and wanted to hire me on the spot. I also knew this was a rather desperate situation, so I was not exactly eager to get involved. I said I would think about it, followed the president to her home, and collected all I needed in order to write the Illinois Arts Council Grant. She left for Florida the next day, and I went home to write the grant and acquire what information I could about the organization from my colleagues in the industry.

I cannot say their remarks were encouraging. They said the music director was "difficult." However, I began to get a sense that the board was not enthusiastic about him and that a future change in the position was possible.

I weighed this information and arrived at the following: I could stick anything out for a year; with the enthusiasm expressed by the board, I might be able to get the deficit down in a short time, since $15,000 wasn't that much; I would be part of a search to hire a new music director, with some say in the decision; and these changes might also include a move to more variety in programming.

After three or four days, I contacted the board president and accepted the position. By the next board meeting, I had submitted the grant and was ready to begin work on the season. I was given the information I needed at the meeting, but before leaving, I asked where I would "hang my hat" when in Woodstock. Since the administrative office space in the Opera House was limited, I was told I would just work at home. I had not intended to make the hour-and-a-half drive to Woodstock on a daily basis anyway.

I understood that my salary would be whatever the Illinois Arts Council Grant produced, since the music director's contracted salary had already been stipulated in the budget. Because of the opportunity to be on the ground floor of formulating a new future for the festival, I agreed to this arrangement. I understood that my own future salary would depend on my efforts and those I could prompt from others.

Before going on, it is important to mention that the Woodstock Opera House is a renowned, historic theatre house. Orson Welles grew up in Woodstock and performed on its stage as a teenager. An important stop on the Summer Stock circuit, the Woodstock Opera House provided opportunities for notables to hone their craft during their developing careers: Paul Newman, Geraldine Page, Shelley Berman, Betsy Palmer, and many others. Because of this historic distinction, the community enthusiastically enjoys and supports its own community theater groups and visiting theater notables.

I was not fully aware of this context as I rapidly began moving ahead with the coming season. However, I soon learned that the community, by and large, did not want the Mozart Festival after the mismanagement and offensive behavior of its former organizers. This outcome was amplified by the fact that the conductor's wife had started the festival for her husband and had tied it to a successful annual theatre event called Woodfest. At the end of the season, which included the new Mozart component, Woodfest was bankrupt and ceased to exist.

But somehow, the Woodstock Mozart Festival continued, and the music director engaged some players from the Rockford Symphony, along with additional high school music students, to comprise a chamber orchestra that would fit on the rather small Opera House stage.

Within weeks, I became aware of the community's animosity toward the festival, so I decided to try to forge a new festival identity through my own involvement. The gifted graphic artist who had designed all the materials for the Fox River Valley Symphony was still available, so I asked him to design a new set of artwork for the Woodstock Mozart Festival.

I sent copies of the new designs to the board president to show as part of my report at the board's March meeting. I was to graduate from the business administration certification course that night in Chicago, so I could not be there. Afterward, she told me the board had voted unanimously to use the former artwork. Because I had not offered the new artwork with the intent of a board vote, but only as a part of my report, I called the treasurer with whom I had dealt to learn what had happened.

He said no one knew anything about the reason for having new artwork and added he doubted anyone cared what artwork was used. I proceeded to have the new designs implemented. That experience provided a glimpse as to the kind of board president I would be dealing with.

I had already seen a preview of her operating style at a meeting with the new managing director of the Opera House, which I also attended. Contract negotiations for the season were the topic, and I was shocked at how aggressive and unreasonable the president and the accompanying board member were. I said little or nothing at the meeting, but the next day I called the managing director to tell him how dismayed I was at their behavior and that this was not going to be my approach in dealing with him and the community. It was clear that major fence mending was required.

The perfect opportunity became available in April when I was sitting in the Opera House office chatting with the two secretaries, who had become friends. A volunteer for the Opera House women's volunteer association was photocopying recipes for that organization's annual spring luncheon fundraising event. We were introduced, and as she spoke with the secretaries, I recognized her accent. I asked where she was from. She said I wouldn't know, as it was a small town in Louisiana. I encouraged her to tell me the name of the town. When she said, "Port Allen," I answered that I had grown up in Baton Rouge. She was surprised. Baton Rouge and Port Allen are located directly across the Mississippi River from each other.

This wonderful, hardworking volunteer is Elizabeth Wester, better known as Beth. She, along with other very dedicated individuals who will be mentioned later, were truly responsible for saving the festival.

Beth and I became friends, and I am grateful to say we still are. We discovered that some of my friends from Baton Rouge High had become her friends in college at LSU. With that she was able to let the community know that I was "okay." In my opinion, this was a "Divine Arrangement," because by now, I knew the community was skeptical about the festival itself, as well as about its new executive director.

It turned out that Beth and her husband, Jim, had lived in the Woodstock area for many years. In fact, their teenage daughter was planning a career in music as a singer. Beth was able to fill me in on many of the details of the festival's history, and at the end of my first season in 1992, she hosted a lovely post-season reception. The point is, it's only later that you realize you have benefitted by a "Divine Arrangement."

After the March 1992 board meeting, all of the festival's administrative and marketing materials were in my possession. The first of the four concerts of the coming sixth season was to feature the music director as pianist and conductor. For the second concert, the soloist was to be an award-winning soprano with a developing career in the U.S. and Europe. The concert master of the New York Philharmonic was to perform during the third concert, and a local chorus in the fourth.

When the president showed me her personally designed budget, with many line items slashed, I informed her that there were no bargains in music rental, instrument cartage and tuning, dues and fees, postage, etc. These were some of the items she had drastically reduced in order to create a budget of $115,000 in expenses. After glancing down the list of line items and knowing what was coming, I told her the real cost of the season would be between $130,000 and $135,000. The final bill at the end of the fiscal year was halfway between those two figures.

By now I had discovered how the previous year's deficit had been reduced to $15,000 from what I finally came to know was originally around $70,000. The executive director and president had "negotiated down" the debt by asking venders to reduce or "forgive" (eliminate) their claims so the festival could survive. One vendor asked if this was called "reverse fundraising."

When the brochures were ready to be mailed, I discovered that this task (together with many others) had been provided by the Opera House staff. With the departure of the former director, these services were no longer available to the festival. We had no funds to hire these necessary services, so I had to do all of them. A sixty-hour workweek became the norm.

Since there were office items I did not have, like a fax machine and copy machine, the board told me to purchase these with the modest funds coming in from donations. Also, we received notice that the amount allocated to the festival for the coming season from the Illinois Arts Council would be $11,000. As mentioned before, this was to be my salary for the year.

When the music director heard about this, he insisted that *he* receive the Arts Council funds as a lump sum payment for the unpaid portion of his salary from the previous year. That was his condition for going ahead with the coming season, for which he expected, in addition, to be paid his full contracted salary.

By this time, tickets were selling, and everyone knew incoming revenues were not going to cover the year's expenses, which included my salary. With this, some board members, including the board president, resigned. Those who remained asked me to stay in good faith and join their efforts to try to turn the festival around.

I spoke briefly with the music director a few times on the phone, but we never met in person before the first rehearsal. The orchestra he had hired was new to him, as he had decided to deal with a Milwaukee contractor who put together a fully professional ensemble. Some of the players were members of the Milwaukee Symphony. This was an artistic upgrade, which sounded good to me.

Unfortunately, the size of the audiences for the singer's performances during the second weekend of the festival were not what the conductor expected. On Saturday night there were eighty-seven persons in the hall, twelve of them Russian sky diving guests of the Opera House's managing director, here on a special skydiving expedition. After the performances on this weekend, the conductor realized his days in Woodstock were over.

This was an alarming circumstance, and a voice inside me was screaming, "You can't let this die!" I had learned through my orchestra administration training that if an orchestra in a small community like Woodstock was discontinued, more than likely it would not be reinstated.

Two doctors on the board were fans of classical music. They were subscribers to the Chicago Symphony and wanted a quality musical product in their community. Another board member had a weekend home in nearby Harvard, Illinois, and wanted to support a cultural event in the area. One of the doctors agreed to be president of the board, and all three wrote checks for $1,000 to enable us to move ahead. The new board president, Dr. Ray Pensinger, then deftly handled the task of notifying the music director that his contract would not be renewed. By now, the board had decided that the festival had to be reduced to a three-weekend event, so I began a search for three guest conductors for the seventh season of 1993.

The League of American Orchestras posted our conductor search information, which eventually resulted in a response of three hundred conductor applicants from all over the world. By this time, I knew we could not afford the Milwaukee players again because I had heard that their union scale was to increase. I looked for a nearby orchestra from which I could hire a chamber orchestra at a reasonable rate. This turned out to be the Elgin Symphony.

Elgin's orchestra contractor was its principal trumpet player, Ross Beacraft.* Through our conversations, I realized that he was deeply knowledgeable about the industry . . . something that as yet I was not! So I asked him to assist me with the search. Clearly, it was to his advantage as well as mine, since we would be using Elgin Symphony players during the coming season.

As the tape recordings came in (there were no CDs yet), Ross suggested I listen and put them in three boxes labeled YES, MAYBE, and NO. I listened day after day, but none of the samples measured up to the level for which I had hoped. It is interesting to note that at this time, no women conductors applied, happily a situation that has by now changed.

In January 1993, I attended a tea for Lady Valerie Solti, whose husband, George Solti, had been music director of the Chicago Symphony. She was in town to raise funds for something, and I was invited to attend the event.

---

* Currently, Ross Beacraft is director of admissions for DePaul University's School of Music in Chicago.

At the tea, I met a young conductor from Vienna who told me he had taken the position as head of the Opera Workshop Department at DePaul University. He had been at the Vienna State Opera as an assistant conductor, and we exchanged business cards. I decided to attend his upcoming performance of *La Bohème*.

I did not look forward to a student performance of this opera, which I had heard many times performed by top professional singers. Furthermore, it was five degrees below zero on this Sunday in February, when I would have preferred a day off. But I went, and as I listened, I was increasingly surprised and amazed by what this young conductor could do with college students. After the performance, I went to the Green Room and invited him to open our coming season. This was my introduction to Karl Sollak.

At the same time, my Louisiana friend Beth Wester had joined the board and had begun planning a spring fundraising brunch event for the festival. Because Beth had been a high-profile, successful volunteer in the Opera House Fine Arts Association, she knew everyone in the community and began to contact those who might be willing to join her in this effort. This was not an easy "sell" for her because the festival was still regarded with suspicion.

As a former home economics major in college, Beth was very familiar with food and food services. She also knew the restaurants in the area, and with her lovely, gracious manner, convinced several chefs to support the festival at the new Chefs' Showcase Brunch. Of course, the opportunity to introduce their culinary samples to a new "audience" was attractive to them as well.

The event took place in the student dining area of McHenry County College, which board members and volunteers magically transformed into a beautiful, spring-like environment. The response from everyone, guests and chefs, was most enthusiastic, and, fortunately, it raised money for the festival.

Chefs' Showcase Brunch Chairman Beth Wester between a Server and Restauranteur Frank Ferru

The seventh season opened on the weekend of July 30–31,1993, with guest conductor Karl Sollak and violinist Eugene Fodor. Although the attendance records no longer exist, I remember that there was a respectable crowd due to renewed interest in the community for experiencing the "new" version of the festival. Eugene Fodor had performed during a prior season and was willing to return for a modest fee. Karl Sollak had not yet appeared in this kind of event in the U.S., so Eugene had to tell him what to wear . . . as he called it, a "frack". . . the German word for what we call tails. Believe it or not, the men in the orchestra had been wearing these very formal, heavy outfits during the previous five summer seasons. Clearly, this was something that needed to change.

Karl Sollak brought new life to the concert hall as he prepared the orchestra. The result was an entirely different dynamic— highly professional and expressively exuberant. As expected, it was completely and appropriately in the style of the composer: moving, convincing, and in good taste. A young Austrian on the podium authenticated the tribute to Mozart's heritage, and Fodor's delivery of Mozart's popular Violin Concerto No. 5 completed the program.

During the second weekend, on August 6–7, pianist and conductor David Schrader was joined by soprano Maria Lagios in Mozart's Concerto for Piano and Voice, "Ch'o mi scordi di te? . . . Non temer." Looking beautiful, Maria appeared in a tea-length pale green gown with sparkles. Together with their superb musical delivery, these two created an experience and scene I have since come to describe as ". . . something out of a Mozart picture book."

Ross Beacraft had suggested inviting a conductor with an established reputation and named three possibilities. One was French Maestra Catherine Comet, who accepted our invitation for the third weekend, and at my suggestion, Ross was featured as soloist in Hummel's Concerto for Trumpet.*

Seeing Ms. Comet's graceful yet energetic style on the podium (in a lovely black gown with swaying skirt) was an entirely new experience for everyone. Also, her husband, Michael Aiken, had

---

* Since Mozart did not write any concertos for trumpet, the Hummel Trumpet Concerto is one that is often programmed, since Hummel was from the same era as Mozart. In fact, child prodigy Johann Nepomuk Hummel actually lived with the Mozart family in order to study with the master. (Mozart 1756–1791; Hummel 1778–1837)

just become Chancellor of the University of Illinois at Urbana-Champaign. She was thrilled to be invited and most complimentary about the charm of the Opera House, the community of Woodstock, and the festival itself. The *Chicago Tribune's* response to her previous appearance with the Chicago Symphony had been, "Let's have her back," and that certainly was our intention.

Now that a vibrant new product had been presented, the festival's board of seven undertook an aggressive fundraising campaign, and audience attendees from the previous season began to respond.

Solicitation letters, a phonathon, direct individual approaches—all were employed. Dr. Pensinger outdid everyone, as he alone raised $25,000. I imagined him in the examining room of his office threatening an undressed patient with confiscating his clothes unless a commitment to support the Mozart Festival was forthcoming. "Whatever works" seemed to be everyone's motto. There was clearly a full-blown, enthusiastic response to the season that motivated the board as plans for the next season evolved.

By the end of the 1993 season, we were in the black, with 36 percent of the deficit erased.

By the time the conductor search ended in 1993, two viable candidates had emerged: Alan Balter, music director of the Memphis Symphony, and Russian conductor Edvard Tchivzhel, an emigrant from St. Petersburg, Russia. I also had received a recommendation from Catherine Cahill, then executive director of the Grant Park Music Festival, in support of a former music school classmate, Kirk Muspratt. At the time, Kirk was an assistant conductor at the Pittsburgh Symphony, and we invited him, Alan Balter, and Catherine Comet for the 1994 season.

The second Chefs' Showcase Brunch was held in the spring of 1994, with increased attendance and financial results. Because it was such a beautiful and appealing affair, the Brunch became an annual event. New, hardworking volunteers were drawn into the effort, many of whom eventually became influential, contributing members of the festival's board.

Early in the summer, before the 1994 season began, I was invited by Chicago's classical music radio station, WFMT, to talk about the festival and the upcoming season. During the half-hour interview with Dennis Moore, Moore periodically interrupted the conversation to mention who I was. "With us today is Anita Whalen, executive director of the Woodstock Mozart Festival." However, at the end of the interview, he said, "We have been talking with Anita Whalen, the artistic director of the Woodstock Mozart Festival."

At the next board meeting, it was clear that everyone had heard the interview. Much to my surprise, Dr. Mark Schiffer, one of the original $1,000 donors, mentioned what Dennis Moore had said at the end of the interview, when I was referred to as the artistic director. I felt that had been a "slip of tongue" and had not thought anything about it. But Dr. Schiffer suggested I should receive that title. I was stunned, not having had any such idea.

Once again, I said, "But I have never done that!" and added that I did not have the skills to develop an orchestra. Unanimously, the board said they did not care, that they did not want a music director, and that they loved the idea of having guest conductors after experiencing the former season. With this, my title was changed to Executive and Artistic Director, and we proceeded with the 1994 season.

A significant publicity opportunity was initiated by patron Marsha Portnoy, a writer, who wrote an article about the festival's recovery for *Craine's Chicago Business*. This article appeared in the July 18th, 1994 edition, just before the season began.

Chicago pianist Chun-Myung Kim was the soloist with Kirk Muspratt during the first weekend; Alan Balter was asked to offer a complete orchestral program during the second weekend; and Catherine Comet returned for the third weekend. All three concerts were memorable, but the final one merits particular attention.

Since Catherine Comet had visited us the year before and knew the quality of Ross Beacraft's playing from his performance of Hummel's Trumpet Concerto, she suggested programming Mozart's *Posthorn Serenade* with him in the solo role. Ross actually owned an authentic reproduction of an original Posthorn, and as a superb player, fulfilled the role impeccably. The audience was enthralled, and at the end of the concert, demanded an encore from the orchestra, which Ms. Comet initiated at the podium. She then walked off the stage, allowing the players to complete on their own the first movement of Mozart's *Eine kleine Nachtmusik*. The audience went wild, and the orchestra players were thrilled. We were off and running!

Chapter 3

SERENADE

During the fall of 1994, I began to plan the 1995 season. Board members often express their desire for one of their favorite selections to be included in the programming, and so it was with Dr. Ray Pensinger, who had been a clarinet student in high school and was fond of Mozart's *Gran Partita Serenade*. This work featured all wind instruments, including two clarinets. I knew Alan Balter was a fine clarinetist, and since he had delivered a fine all-orchestral performance as conductor the year before, I invited him to return. I asked him to include the *Serenade* in his concert and to participate in it as one of the clarinetists.

Because Karl Sollak had been a hit during the 1993 season, we invited him to return during the second weekend with a young Austrian pianist he recommended, Barbara Moser. I also invited the other conductor we favored during the conductor's search, Edvard Tchivzhel, for the third weekend.

I wanted to engage a violinist as a soloist during this weekend, and since I enjoyed Viktoria Mullova's playing, I called her New York agent, Pat Winter, at ICM (now Opus 3 Artists). Pat told me Viktoria wouldn't be in the U.S. during 1995, so featuring her would not be possible.

It is important to mention here that it might seem impossible for a small operation like the Woodstock Mozart Festival to entertain the idea of engaging a world-class European artist like Viktoria Mullova. Clearly, for us, her fee and travel expenses would be unaffordable. I was aware that I was overreaching; however, I am also a firm believer in the adage, "Nothing ventured, nothing gained."*

Since it was not going to be possible to engage Mullova, Winter suggested another New York-based violinist whom she said was a wonderful interpreter of Mozart. His name was Mark Peskanov. I had never heard Mark's playing, but took her word for it. I did know about his pianist brother, Alexander Peskanov. She mentioned that Mark Peskanov had played all the big houses around the world, naming a few. I asked if she thought he would be interested in coming to such small place. She said she thought he would enjoy it as a "change of pace." She asked him, he agreed, and we engaged violinist Mark Peskanov, together with conductor Edvard Tchivzhel for the final weekend of the 1995 festival.

I must add that when Mark arrived and looked around inside the Opera House hall he exclaimed, "I love this!"

Back to the opening weekend's programming of Mozart's *Gran Partita Serenade* as mentioned above.

Although I willingly and happily wanted to reward Dr. Pensinger for his contributions on behalf of helping to save the

---

* It does happen that when an international artist from Europe or Asia performs with a major U.S. arts organization, they are willing to add another concert at a nearby, lesser-known venue as well for a more modest fee.

festival, I had reservations about featuring this work. I knew the audience we were serving was probably not used to the sound of an all-wind ensemble. Furthermore, as a compositional form, serenades were written more as background music with several movements, which to some listeners can become tedious. I was surprised and delighted when a group of farmers reserved a substantial block of tickets for the concert.

Despite my reservations, we went ahead with programming the *Serenade* during the opening weekend's performances. Alan Balter played the principal clarinet part and, between the movements, gave the most delightful and entertaining short talks, to which the audience responded enthusiastically . . . especially the farmers! Karl Sollak and pianist Barbara Moser were a hit during the second weekend, and conductor Edvard Tchivzhel with violinist Mark Peskanov in Mozart's Violin Concerto No. 3 literally blew the roof off the Opera House during the final weekend. What a run!

Most endearing to the audience was Mark's sitting in with the second violin section during the second half of the concert after playing his concerto during the first half. I came to know later, during our years of partnership, that the evening's featured symphony, Mozart's Symphony No. 40, had been his favorite as a child.

The audience recognized his generosity of spirit (and love of music) by his spontaneously volunteering to participate in that performance in the back of the violin section, and not as a featured soloist.

⌒

By the 1995 season, another change in orchestra personnel had become necessary. The Elgin Symphony had raised its rate for the use of its players, and the Milwaukee Symphony had eliminated its summer services due to an increase in union fees. As a result, we could no longer afford Elgin players, but the Milwaukee players were willing to accept what we could afford due to the elimination of their summer performances.

With this change came a new and wonderful association with Milwaukee contractor Lori Babinec.

I did not know it at the time, but from this point on, I no longer needed to be concerned about my lack of ability to "build" an orchestra. Lori, who also served as our principal bassoonist and librarian, was my right-hand partner in this necessary and important pursuit. A woman of many talents and abilities, she had previously served as assistant librarian for the Milwaukee

Lori Babinec, Personnel Manager and Principal Bassoon

Symphony and as a substitute player in that orchestra. Not only was she our orchestra's musician's contractor and librarian, she also fulfilled these roles for many other Milwaukee-based groups. You could say she knew her way around.

Lori was efficient and accurate at everything she did. She possessed a unique wisdom about the dynamics of selecting and inviting players that enabled the orchestra to improve over the years. Bonuses included her agreeable, generous personality and availability whenever there was a need, even when solicited requests required time and effort above and beyond the call of duty.

Together, we agreed upon the most important underlying dynamics for the highest level of music making. These included compatibility of the abilities and personalities of the players, and a strong code of respect for all involved. Our conviction about this extended to conductors and soloists as well. We simply did not tolerate rude or abusive behavior among the players or from the podium. These were our first considerations for hiring anyone.

Although I had been assigned the artistic responsibility by the board, I remained fully aware that I had never done any such thing except choose teaching materials for my former piano students. I also knew that every conductor was an artistic director by virtue of his or her position. Clearly, any soloists we might engage also were quite knowledgeable due to their professional roles and experiences.

Thanks to Lori's detailed record keeping, we always had an up-to-date list of repertoire performed through the years. Each conductor who agreed to guest conduct received a copy of the list and a request for three possible programs. All were accustomed to keeping costs in check, so this was seldom a problem once budgetary parameters were indicated. The soloist was asked for his or her selection, which was also conveyed to the conductor. After the necessary discussions, an agreement was reached. This seems like a simple process, and it was, because all those involved were highly professional.

Talent, knowledge, experience, inspiration, intuition, and mutual respect were all essential ingredients.

By this time a prominent and influential person in the community had joined the board and had become its vice president,

Charie Zanck, president of the Amcore Bank. Charie offered her staff's assistance with developing a database in order to launch a new fundraising effort called The Mozart Festival Society. Beautiful invitations were sent asking individuals to join at the $250 level and corporate members at the $750 level. For these commitments, members were to be invited to a private black-tie reception, be recognized in the season program booklet, and receive a Mozart Festival Society lapel pin. The purpose of the memberships was also indicated:

> *Your annually renewable membership will help assure the continuation of the rich musical experience provided by the Woodstock Mozart Festival. Please join us in this effort.*

Charie and her husband Tom hosted one of the black-tie receptions in their beautiful home, as did others in their lovely homes over the years.

Forty-five individual members joined the Society during the first year, as well as five corporations. Furthermore, the third board member, who had originally offered $1,000 in 1993, began underwriting one of the three concerts with his wife at the $2,500 level, as did a corporation and a bank. These were Jon and Linda Ender; Aptargroup, Inc. with the Aptargroup Foundation; and the Amcore Foundation. We also gained fifty-five program advertisers, and twenty-three restaurants participated in the spring Chefs' Showcase Brunch that demonstrated the chefs' culinary skills.

In addition, we presented our first Family Concert in October 1995 featuring the Chicago Youth Symphony Orchestra's Encore Chamber Orchestra.

Maestra Catherine Comet

Maestro Edvard Tchivzhel, Anita Whalen, and Violinist
Mark Peskanov after the concert

Tom and Charie Zanck, Anita Whalen, and Dr. Ray Pensinger,
Board President

By 1996, the deficit had been erased, and we had a small surplus.
In addition to the other fundraising initiatives, several board and
audience members had voluntarily increased their donations to
$1,000—as well as one to $2,500 and another to $5,000.

My husband, Charlie, and I hosted a Louisiana-style dinner
party for the key board members responsible for this important
achievement. It was the first of many such parties over the years
featuring a variety of cuisines to show our appreciation to major
festival contributors. Thanks to my mother, who had been called
the "Perle Mesta* of the Baton Rouge Symphony League," I had

---

* "Perle Mesta was an American political hostess and U.S. ambassador to
Luxembourg. She was known for her lavish parties for Washington, DC,
society. Attendees also included artists, entertainers, and many national
political figures." (Wikipedia)

learned how to do this kind of entertaining. I always loved to cook, and luckily, Charlie was an excellent host.

In keeping with Mozart's birthplace, we asked Austrian Airlines to assist with our fundraising effort by offering a trip as a raffle prize. They generously obliged with a trip to Vienna that included two business-class tickets and three nights' lodging at the Radisson SAS Palais Hotel. The winners of the trip could extend their stay at their own expense. Raffle tickets were inserted in all the program books.

We were very grateful to Austrian Airlines and their delightful representative, Karen Kanzia, who, for many years visited the final performances of the festival to draw the winning raffle ticket, with an accompanying drum roll. Thanks to the Geneva Inn in Lake Geneva, Wisconsin, we were also able to offer a second prize Weekend Getaway for Two at this beautiful resort.

By this time, two florists had become involved in the festival: John Molthen, of Apple Creek Flowers, and Betty Thomas, of Busse Thomas Flowers and Gifts. It is important to mention how helpful and generous these two were in many ways for many years.

John, whose shop also included a gift area, had undertaken the project of selecting, ordering, and managing Mozart memorabilia: t-shirts and sweatshirts, mugs, Mozart candies, pens, key rings, and so on. He artfully displayed these on tables in the Community Room where people gathered during intermissions. To enhance the environment further, Betty generously provided magnificent floral pieces. The walls of the Community Room were always graced with the works of local artists, making it an especially inviting place where refreshments could be purchased.

The Woodstock Opera House

Most important was the attraction of the Opera House itself. Situated on the picturesque town square featuring a gazebo, the 1880s Woodstock Opera House had been authentically restored. The beauty and charm of the Steamboat Gothic style building were clearly a major draw for out-of-town visitors. Local residents were also rightfully very proud of their treasure, which has been placed on the National Historic Register.

The aural and visual effects of the performances inside the hall were also dramatic and captivating assets. Because there were only 412 seats in the hall, and because of the horseshoe-shaped wrap-around balcony, audiences felt embraced by the sound. The proximity to the artists magnified the impact of the performances in a way not possible in a larger venue. This was a unique effect, one which many commented on over the years, even saying, "I would rather attend a concert there than in a large hall." Clearly, this was an advantage.

During 1996, conductor Catherine Comet returned with pianist Janis Vakarelis; Karl Sollak with Donald Peck, principal flutist of the Chicago Symphony; and Edvard Tchivzhel with Mark Peskanov. An hour before each concert, half-hour Conductor/Artist Conversations were offered in the Community Room. These popular introductions became the norm.

The Woodstock Opera House

Catherine Comet, music director of the Grand Rapids (Michigan) Symphony, was accustomed to these conversations, and Janis Vakarelis seemed comfortable with them as well.

The format included discussions about the concert repertoire, followed by questions and answers from the audience. Austrian conductor Sollak was concerned that his command of English might not be up to the task, so Norm Pellegrini, WFMT* radio's producer/host of the Chicago Symphony and Lyric Opera Broadcasts, was invited to interview him and assist with the questions and answers.

Edvard Tchivzhel addressed the pre-concert conversation audience alone because violin soloist Peskanov was not fond of "talking."

In preparation for the 1997 season, it is important to relate the following:

During a rehearsal break before the final weekend's performances, we were in a local restaurant waiting for our lunch to arrive. It was taking a long time, and there was a console piano right next to our table. Edvard and Mark began joking, wondering if the piano "worked." Edvard's wife and eleven-year-old son were with us, and the two men tried to get the son to play something on the piano to see if it "worked." True to their natures, both men were boisterous. Aware that this was an embarrassing situation for an eleven-year-old, I got up and played a Chopin waltz.

The two men applauded and howled: "BRAVO, you practiced!" which I nonchalantly waved off. On the way back to the Opera House, Mark said he wanted me to play with him. I was flabbergasted and said I'd kill myself before doing that.

---

* WFMT 98.7 is Chicago's classical music radio station.

By 1997 the board had grown to fourteen members, and by then I was receiving a respectable salary. Our mailings were handled by a service, but I was still responsible for all other administrative tasks (marketing, grant writing, financial, fundraising, etc.). The Mozart Festival Society and Chefs' Showcase Brunch continued to grow in attendance and membership, and the resulting increase in revenues enabled us to begin saving small surpluses.

Three significant artistic developments occurred in 1997. One was the engagement of the new principal oboist of the Chicago Symphony, Alex Klein, as soloist. Due to the publicity preceding and following Alex's new assignment, we were anticipating a very special concert, and for this we were richly rewarded. Alex is an exceptional artist, and his performance of Mozart's Oboe Concerto was an unforgettable experience.

The second new artistic arrangement was Mark Peskanov's serving as violinist *and* conductor. It is not an uncommon role for instrumentalists to serve as both soloist and conductor; in this case, however, Mark also brought a partner to join him in Mozart's Sinfonia Concertante for Violin and Viola. The partner was a cellist, Daniel Gaisford, who had transcribed the viola part for cello.

The third new artistic arrangement occurred when musical introductions were substituted for two of the pre-concert conversations. The first of these was held during the opening weekend with a performance of Mozart's "Kegelstatt" Trio featuring pianist Richard Ormrod, clarinetist Alan Balter (also the evening's conductor), and violist Robert Levine.

Since Mark did not want to "talk" before his concerts during the third weekend, he insisted that I play with him, just as he had suggested the previous year after the restaurant experience. There seemed to be no alternative, so we played a Mozart sonata for piano and violin before his 1997 concert, the first of many collaborations. These were wonderful opportunities for me, the former "performance" major in college who just "knew" she would never be a "performer"!

———

The year 1998 was our tenth season. We had continued to feature all-Mozart programming. It was becoming obvious that in addition to my own preference for more variety, there were signs from supporters that they wanted to expand the festival's artistic horizons. Major donor and concert underwriter John Ender, who had been attending the festival since its inception, actually told me, "If I hear the Jupiter Symphony one more time, I am going to withdraw my support!"

We knew of several Mozart festivals with mixed programming, Mostly Mozart, OK Mozart, and others. However, we really did not want to change our name. Good friend Gene Medford offered the solution. His suggestion was not to change our name, but to add the byline "Mozart . . . and More!" We further indicated that our efforts would include "More Composers; More Music; More Fun!"

In keeping with the "More Composers" feature, conductor David Loebel led the orchestra and assisted cellist Daniel Gaisford, who was a hit as soloist in Haydn's C Major Cello Concerto during the first weekend. For the pre-concert introduction, I prepared a short talk about "Mozart as a Mason," since Mozart's Freemason membership was an important influence in his life. Then Daniel and I played Beethoven's 12 Variations on a Theme from Mozart's opera, *The Magic Flute,* which includes Masonic symbolism.

As an outgrowth of the pre-concert musical introductions during the preceding two years, and to follow up with "More Music," we offered two Saturday afternoon chamber music concerts. One was an April co-sponsored event with the Woodstock Fine Arts Association (a support group of the Opera House), as part of their "Music for a Sunday Afternoon" series. The other was a prelude to the final weekend's festival concert.

Tickets for these separate, albeit shorter, Saturday afternoon concerts could be purchased separately at a lower rate. We felt it would be a beneficial option for families who wanted to take their children to a concert and for seniors who did not want to drive at night.

Since Mark Peskanov did not wish to participate in the pre-concert discussions, he and his pianist brother, Alex, were instead featured in this chamber music concert, along with members of the orchestra in Mozart's Quartet in E-flat for Violin, Cello and Piano. After a short intermission, the audience enjoyed Mendelssohn's Octet in E-flat Major, making it a blockbuster concert. That evening, Alex played Mozart's Piano Concerto No. 14, and the orchestra performed Mendelssohn's Concerto for String Orchestra, making it another blockbuster event.

So as not to alarm our faithful Mozart enthusiasts, we invited Hans Graf to conduct an all-Mozart orchestral concert during the second weekend. Following is an explanation of how this happened.

The year before, on my drive to Woodstock, I had heard some Mozart Dances and Marches on the FM radio. I remember thinking how "perfect" they sounded. The radio announcer said they'd been played by the Mozarteum Orchestra under the direction of Hans Graf. Clearly, this orchestra, based in Salzburg,* was where one should be able to hear "perfect" Mozart, and Hans Graf was well known to musicians by his reputation.

Since we had saved money from the festival's years of small surpluses, I called Maestro Graf's agent in San Francisco, the legendary Mariedi Anders. As expected, his fee and flight requirements were beyond those of the conductors we had invited to date. Furthermore, board members were unfamiliar with him since he had not appeared in Chicago. It was not easy to convince them that it was important for us to feature him. Eventually, they agreed.

As for "More Fun," I will never forget how I introduced him to the audience assembled for the pre-concert talk: "We are delighted to have with us this weekend, conductor Hans Graf from Salzburg . . . just like Coke, the real thing!" He burst out laughing, and the audience joined him, as did I, since I had very much surprised myself with my spontaneity. We were off to a great beginning followed by an equally great concert. The board was thrilled and afterward agreed that Graf's visit had enabled us to "raise the bar."

---

* Salzburg, Austria, Mozart's birthplace

Chapter 4

CONCERTO

The 1998 Season was not only a milestone for the festival artistically, it also allowed us to increase our audience. One hundred additional attendees had responded to the mixed programming of "Mozart . . . and More!" Also, by now the board had developed a mission statement:

> *To inspire and educate audiences of all ages through a chamber orchestral program of an outstanding caliber which is centered on Mozart.*

All agreed that the works of composers considered for mixed programming should be by composers who had influenced or been influenced by Mozart. However, as visiting clarinetist Charles Neidich pointed out the following year, "All composers who preceded Mozart influenced him, and all who followed were influenced by him." Over time, this insight became the basis for continuing to provide fresh, exciting programming.

Charles's appearance with us during the 1999 season was enabled by Mark Peskanov, who had by then been named the festival's artistic advisor. Following is an explanation of how this came to be.

Aware that I had not been trained as an artistic director, I had continued to be concerned about my ability (good luck?) at finding artists and conductors who were of the quality with which we had been graced. I mentioned often to board members over the prior six years that I hoped to find a partner to assist with this important function, someone in the industry connected to an array of effective performers.

I didn't immediately recognize it, but a possible partner had already appeared—Mark Peskanov. We definitely seemed to be "on the same wavelength," and his generous, fun-loving, spontaneous creative spirit was a bonus. He was not only practical, but also VERY experienced. As an active performer, he had collaborated with many world-class orchestras and artists.

From his 1999 Mozart Festival program bio:

Mr. Peskanov has performed with the New York Philharmonic, as well as with the orchestras of Montreal, Vancouver, Louisville, Cincinnati, Tucson, Buffalo, and Phoenix. He has toured Japan with the NHK Orchestra of Tokyo under the direction of Wolfgang Sawallisch and also appeared with the Philadelphia and Cleveland Orchestras, the Los Angeles Philharmonic, the St. Louis, Chicago, Minnesota, San Francisco and National Symphonies as well as with the London Philharmonic.

As recitalist and ensemble player, Mark Peskanov has collaborated with artists such as Isaac Stern, Yo-Yo Ma and

Yefim Bronfman. He performs frequently with the Chamber Music Society of Lincoln Center and in the unique New York Barge Music chamber concerts for which he also serves as an Artistic Director.

His appearances at music festivals include the Amsterdam Concertgebouw Chamber Music Festival, as well as those of Aspen, Boulder, Grant Park, the Hollywood Bowl, Meadowbrook, Tanglewood, and Wolf Trap. Mark Peskanov was named Artistic Advisor to the Woodstock Mozart Festival in 1998.

Mark's involvement as one of six artistic directors with New York's Barge Music was a unique attribute that fit nicely with our circumstances. Usually, artistic directors bear the title alone, so sharing the responsibility was important to our situation. With my having fulfilled the role to date, the board did not suggest I relinquish it. Basically, we were to be partners, and under the circumstances, I assumed the title of General Director.

Most important is that we shared the same intent: to bring great joy to audience members and to inspire them, not only to love classical music, but also to have a wonderful time, to be entertained, and to be moved by the performances. Over time, we were richly rewarded.

Mark knew an array of artists available in New York and in Europe. He had his finger on the pulse of whatever was the latest in the industry worldwide. Sometimes, I thought he was endowed with special antennae.

Here is what Board President Ray Pensinger wrote about Mark in his 1999 program letter to the audience: "His stature as a musician, his knowledge of programming as to 'what works,' and his enthusiasm will continue to be an invaluable benefit to the festival in years to come."

It was through Mark that we were able to engage clarinetist Charles Neidich for our 1999 season. Neidich's performances of Mozart's Clarinet Quintet and Clarinet Concerto were unforgettable.

It is worth mentioning a related event that followed. My parents had moved back to Baton Rouge during their retirement, and my dad had rejoined the Baton Rouge Symphony board. I had sent them a copy of our program book after the season, and at a Symphony concert in the fall, my mother showed it to the orchestra's artistic administrator. She was amazed to see Charles as one of our guest artists and said, "How did they get him? No one can get him!"

Clarinetist Charles Neidich

By this time, I also had discovered New York agents who understood our needs and who were able to connect us with visiting artists and conductors. It is worth mentioning Harry Bicket, a young British conductor who had come to Chicago a few days before his engagement with us to speak with Lyric Opera management. When he arrived in Woodstock he told me he had gone there to discuss plans for an opera he was to conduct in four years. When the *Chicago Tribune* called to ask me about our 1999 season, they wondered who Harry Bicket was and where he had been engaged, because they had not heard of him. I mentioned the various venues in his bio, but will skip ahead from there.

By now opera fans know that Harry has conducted at the Metropolitan Opera in New York and at other important opera houses. He is also music director of The English Concert and of the Santa Fe Opera. At his 1999 concert with us, Harry collaborated with Chicago Symphony principal flutist Donald Peck and principal harpist Sarah Bullen in Mozart's Flute and Harp Concerto, making it another special event.

Our experience with Harry convinced me that even with our constrained financial resources, the festival could gain a reputation for engaging guest conductors and artists who were "on their way up."

Also by 1999, two important new members had joined the orchestra. One was a colleague of Mark's, cellist Eugene Osadchy. At the time a member of the Vancouver Symphony, Eugene was invited to help strengthen the bass section. He was with us for three summers.

The second "imported" musician was string bassist Peter Nelson, who joined the orchestra while visiting his in-laws, festival supporters Joan and Charles Whitney of Batavia, Illinois, during the summer. Peter's career had taken him to Germany, where he was a member of a regional orchestra, and he also was able to connect us to a few conductors he had come to know.

As a member of an ensemble from his German orchestra, Peter and his colleagues presented concerts of rediscovered turn-of-the-century European caféhaus musik. This popular group, the Thüringer Salonquintett, was on tour in the U.S. in February, and for us they presented two events: a Saturday afternoon Family Concert featuring Camille Saint Saëns's Carnival of the Animals, and a Sunday Valentine's Day Viennese Garden Party fundraising event. Both were charming and enthusiastically received. However, as a warning, we discovered that featuring special events in February was not a good idea, since many of our patrons were away visiting warmer climes during that time.

Louise LeCoque was the newly elected president of the festival board in 2000. Dr. Ray Pensinger had served generously and effectively as the festival's president for seven years and had wisely guided us through many challenges. He was now ready to "pass the baton" to Louise, a strong and generous supporter.

Having been active and instrumental in the Chefs' Showcase Brunch, Louise had taken charge of the silent auction, which she had expanded, offering desirable and valuable items. The resulting revenue from her efforts was remarkable. As board president, she was able to apply her talents to increasing both attendance and financial support for the festival.

During the prior six years, Louise and her husband, Erv, had served as major forces "behind the scenes." Because of their extended influence as members of the nearby community of Crystal Lake, the festival received increased exposure and support. As president of the Aptargroup Corporation, Erv's connections enabled them to host an introductory presentation about the festival for McHenry County corporations. His good friend Bob Blazier, president of the Crystal Lake Chamber of Commerce, arranged another of these for the McHenry County Economic Development Corporation. The LeCoques secured two important concert sponsorships from which the festival benefitted for several years: Home State Bank and Sage Products. The Aptargroup Foundation itself continued to support the festival as a concert underwriter, as did the LeCoques themselves. In addition, Louise and Erv graciously and generously hosted beautiful celebratory post-concert dinner parties at the close of many seasons for artists, board members, and special guests.

An important point is that several others not previously mentioned also played vital roles in the festival's success.

Jim Wester's efforts in assisting his wife, Beth, with the Chefs' Showcase Brunch was invaluable. Jim had been educated as an engineer. His ability to invent and actually make items necessary for the festival event was amazing. With his infectious personality and experience as an airline pilot, he was a popular announcer at the Brunch. Jim also documented concerts and events with memorable photos with his camera.

Dr. Pensinger's wife, Lynn, often hostessed dinners for the artists in their lovely home. My husband, Charlie, an attorney, wrote all contracts and monitored the festival's legal matters. The women on the board and wives of the male board members assumed major responsibilities, either with the Brunch and/or with fundraising. Clarice Caufield secured the support of Harris Bank. She and her husband Farlin became generous concert underwriters who enjoyed hosting artists at post-concert dinners.

All board members contributed financially to the festival, as well as to the brunches, by donating and soliciting items for the auction. This was done with amazing generosity and enthusiasm, which pervaded the atmosphere. The festival had become an annual event welcomed by growing audiences.

The 2000 season was again marked by wonderful performances. Mark Peskanov appeared as violinist and conductor and enabled us to engage pianist Gerald Robbins for another weekend. With his solo performance, principal cellist Eugene Osadchy completed his three-year festival residency, by now having accomplished his charge of strengthening the bass section of the orchestra. At my invitation, hornist James Sommerville also appeared.

I had hoped to invite a special French horn player as soloist, and again, as I was driving to Woodstock during the previous year, I was listening to the FM radio. I heard a wonderful recording of one of Mozart's horn concertos, a new release, and at the end of the performance I listened carefully for the names of the soloist and orchestra. I caught the CBC (Canadian Broadcasting Company) Orchestra part, but only "Summer" something for the artist.

So I called Eugene Osadchy at home in Vancouver. He was not there, but his wife Elena answered the phone, and she knew immediately who the horn player was, James Sommerville. She said Eugene had been the principal cellist of the CBC Orchestra on the day the recording was made and that "Jamie" had played right through all six Mozart horn concertos with practically no retakes, just "like falling off a log." The natural ease of his performance was evident in what I'd heard on the radio. I discovered through his Canadian agent that James had just been named principal hornist of the Boston Symphony, and we were able to engage him. We were indeed rewarded with very special performances of Mozart Horn Concertos 1 and 4.

Erv LeCoque and Board President Louise LeCoque

Principal cellist Eugene Osadchy, and Farlin and Clarice Caufield
with Maestro Hans Graf

A wonderful, timely arrangement occurred in 2001 when CPA Ed Streit joined the board. Although an excellent accounting firm had been providing monthly services, a professional accountant on the board, to serve as treasurer, was a welcome opportunity. In this role, Ed became an invaluable member of the management team. During 2001 two board members generously began to contribute $10,000 each: Jon and Linda Ender and Geraldine Grennan. Others also voluntarily raised the level of their contributions, some to $5,000, others to $2,500, $1,000, and so forth. Clearly, Ed was able to assist with managing these new circumstances, as well as to serve as a sounding board for me. His easy-going and professionally supportive manner was a bonus.

Jon and Linda Ender

All other ongoing activities continued to be successful, and the first weekend of the 2001 season got off on a high note with the young, handsome Greek duo-pianists Petrou and Apostolopoulos.

Under the direction of British conductor Russell Harris, they brought the house down with Mozart's Concerto for Two Pianos followed by a surprise "Boogie, Woogie" encore. Mozart would have loved it!

Soprano Helen Donath gave an amazing performance, which included Mozart's "Exultate, Jubilate," and her conductor husband, Klaus, provided a beautiful interpretation of our first Schubert Symphony, No. 5. Many opera buffs came out to Woodstock from Chicago (sixty miles away) to hear Helen because of her reputation. However, we learned through this third engagement of a singer that singers were not as popular with our Woodstock audience as instrumentalists.

Geraldine Grennan and Artistic Advisor Mark Peskanov

Mark Peskanov was joined by orchestra members for the second year in the Chamber Music Concert, held during the third festival weekend. This arrangement became the norm. Mark also played Bach's Concerto for Two Violins with concertmaster

Karen Smith. These were important opportunities for the musicians in the orchestra to personally perform every year with an artist of Mark's level in small groups and duo performances. Over time, the practice enabled the players to become better musicians and better at playing together, which enhanced the orchestra's reputation.

In terms of "building" the orchestra, the usual method of auditioning for open seats was not employed. As mentioned in an earlier chapter, personnel manager Lori Babinec had a knack for engaging players who worked well together and were personally compatible. The same people returned each year, and the players began to tell us that the festival was their "favorite place to play." This was important in the long-term for building a progressively more cohesive and effective team.

If a seat in the orchestra became vacant because someone moved away, Mark suggested asking the person next to that seat to "bring a friend"—someone they enjoyed playing with. As a result, the group became exceptionally congenial, the atmosphere warm and accepting. It is so important for players to be able to trust one another, because being an orchestra musician is one of the most stressful careers.

The necessary precision when participating requires that players be consistently alert, with unyielding concentration. Sensitivity to the conductor's directives and to everything else happening around them is necessary for an inspired result. When it is time for them to play, their entry must be at the precise time with the appropriate expression. The inability to correct possible mishaps makes music performance akin to "living on the edge."

The festival orchestra was unique and did become exceptional because of the congenial, trusting atmosphere among the players. By contrast, most orchestras hire members through auditioning. Members of an orchestra can actually "challenge" those seated "above" them, hoping to move up in the ranks. This can create a competitive atmosphere rather than one of acceptance and cooperation, and there is always the risk of clashing personalities. This is difficult to identify during the auditioning process.

Two other dynamics influenced the orchestra's development in Woodstock. One was that the group had a different conductor each week during the festival's three-week consecutive run. The other was due to the financial restrictions necessary for presenting quality performances to a small audience.

Each week's rehearsals were limited to only three services.* The result was a flexible, nimble orchestra that could "turn on a dime." To say the group became a "crack" ensemble over the twenty plus years that many of them were together is not an exaggeration. It is truly unusual for the core members of an orchestra to be consistently together for as long a period as this orchestra came to be.

<hr />

The year 2002 was again a time of new developments.

On Wednesday evenings before the weekend concerts, the orchestra's new AMADEUS HARMONIE wind octet presented

---

* In orchestral terms, a "service" is either a rehearsal or a performance. Players are paid by the service, and each service is an exact length of time. The orchestra contractor/personnel manager is in charge of announcing the precise beginning and end times for a rehearsal (even if the players are in the middle of playing a phrase or the conductor in the middle of a sentence). However, there is more flexibility for performances, the timing of which cannot be so rigidly controlled.

free concerts in the Gazebo in the Park as a gift to the community. These popular events continued for several years.

Mark Peskanov and Anita Whalen on Anita's 10th Anniversary
with the Festival

During the festival itself, of note was the appearance of pianist Jeremy Menuhin (son of Yahudi Menuhin) during the first weekend. It was my tenth season with the festival. For this anniversary, Mark and the orchestra performed Sarasate's "Zigeunerweisen" (Gypsy Airs) in honor of my Hungarian heritage during his weekend of concerts. The inclusion of this lighter work as part of the program was so enthusiastically received that from then on, similar lighter works were programmed.

Thinking ahead to 2003 . . .

During the prior few years, attendance at Friday evening concerts had been gradually diminishing, enough to prompt consideration of a change. We noticed that many of the retirees at our evening performances were no longer with us, either having moved to be near their children or no longer able to drive at night. The solution was to change the Friday/Saturday evening schedule to Saturday evenings/Sunday afternoons. This change offered the option for retirees and others to attend a matinee performance on Sundays.

Another way in which we hoped to increase attendance was through a group sales program. To devise and implement the program, we hired a group sales representative, Lila Keleher, from Naperville.

I had known Lila casually for years. While coincidentally meeting in the check-out line at the grocery store, I asked how she was. She said she was fine and had recently retired from Lucent Technologies. She added that she enjoyed being retired during the fall and holidays, but that boredom was setting in now that it was January. Knowing what a capable, multitalented person Lila was, I mentioned the need for a group sales program for the festival. A few days later, she agreed to undertake the task.

Lila researched the retirement communities in the west and northwest suburbs, designed introductory materials, and, with her graphic arts capabilities, even created our season brochures. In the 2002 program, we announced our new schedule of Saturday and Sunday afternoon concerts for 2003 and encouraged our elderly patrons and those with young families to consider attending the Sunday afternoon performance:

Make a Date with Lila!

It's not too early to make plans for our 2003 season showcasing music that invites, inspires and surprises! Lila

Keleher, Director of Audience Development, can assist you in creating a group outing to the Woodstock Mozart Festival. Let the music and the history-rich surroundings transport you back in time. Take a walking tour of Woodstock's historic landmarks, explore the charming boutiques on Woodstock's Town Square and enjoy dining in an area restaurant. Let's make a date—same time next year!

Lila Keleher

For group rates, reservations and information, contact Lila Keleher at. . . .

Chapter 5

SYMPHONY

With *Mark on board*, performance practices continued as described. Guest artists and conductors were invited; some orchestra players appeared with Mark or as duo-soloists. Together with orchestra players, I also played in the chamber music concerts.

Some may have thought that preparing for the festival began in the spring, and after the summer performances, activities were suspended until the following spring. In fact, planning and running each event was more than a year-long effort with artist and conductor searches beginning at least two years in advance. Following the summer's performances, it was important for

Daniel Campbell, former Box Office Manager, now Opera House Managing Director

the board and management to review and assess the season. The Opera House became an important contributor to this evaluation process, especially its box office manager, Daniel Campbell.

Daniel was an invaluable ally and influence for many reasons. Trained as a classical singer with a degree in music, he understood everything about our operation. Day by day, he could see what was selling and what was not. He also knew the community and heard remarks made by patrons as they purchased tickets. Through this, we both learned a lot that enabled us to keep our "finger on the pulse."

GENERAL SCHEDULE:

SEPTEMBER:
Evaluation of the season and engagement of artists and conductors for the following year, as well as confirmation of programming.

OCTOBER:
Listening/editing season CDs for sending as year-end appreciation gifts to major corporate and individual donors.

NOVEMBER:
Newsletter to patrons recognizing individuals for their efforts during the season with an introduction to next year's season. Corporate appeals sent before Thanksgiving; year-end appeals sent to patrons the day after Thanksgiving.

DECEMBER:
Conductors and artists under signed contract.

JANUARY:
Subscription renewal brochures mailed on the 3rd and 31st.

FEBRUARY
Brochures for new subscriptions mailed February 14.

MARCH:
Repeat mailing of brochures for new subscriptions mailed March 14. Fundraising Phone-a-thon completed.

APRIL:
Single ticket brochures and program ad forms.

MAY:
Festival Spring Newsletters and Opera House Summer Season brochures, which included the festival schedule. Publications press releases to *New York Times*, *Midwest Living Magazine*, *Chicago Magazine*, and others.

JUNE:
Brochures mailed to lists previously arranged through "list swaps" with other Illinois and Wisconsin orchestras.

JULY:
After July 4th weekend, press releases sent to news publications, radio, and TV stations. Resulting newspaper articles and radio interviews about the upcoming season occurred because of the press releases. Radio ads were also aired during the final weeks before the performance weekends.

Obviously, the various efforts were overlapping during the year. A *Chicago Tribune* feature prized by all music performance organizations was to be listed in the "Picks of the Week" column each Friday. We were blessed with many such listings, often for all three weekends of concerts.

～

During the 2003 season, attendance began to drop. The addition of a chamber music concert in 2004 helped make up the difference, but in 2005 there was another reduction in total ticket revenues. Together, these created a $12,000 reduction in ticket sales. However, by then it was clear that attendance had gradually been on the decline since the end of the 1990s, when all concerts had been selling out, not only for us, but also for other orchestras.

I had not been to a League of American Orchestras Conference for some years, and in the materials about the 2006 National Conference, a seminar was scheduled about a new marketing approach by an outfit called Target Research Group Arts, or TRG. I signed up to attend the conference in Los Angeles in June 2006.

At the seminar, I learned about the new marketing approach called "Analytics." Like many other orchestras, at that time we lacked the staff and funds to track patrons' attendance.

However, I learned that TRG was advising many orchestras around the country, not only about this data collection process, but also about other matters, including the most effective approach to designing and disseminating brochures. Since we had been using the designs of our graphic artist, it seemed now was the time to try additional marketing approaches.

On December 1, 2006, TRG consultant Joanne Steller came for a day to advise us on all marketing material matters. We spent an intense time together, including a meeting with board members who could make it on a snowy day. What an eye-opener her suggested changes were, down to the most effective words to use to sell subscriptions and single tickets. I still see these same words and details in brochures of major orchestras, all of which I am sure have TRG on retainer.

Joanne helped us rescale the House and raise prices, reduce the number of complimentary tickets by half, apply an across-the-board 10 percent discount to subscribers, set a specific goal of $80,000 in ticket sales, and brief the box office staff on how to make suggestions. "If you like [something], you will really like this." When a customer asks about the first concert, the box office suggests that they also consider the third concert. This is called "up-selling."

A new schedule of mailing the redesigned brochures was also an important part of the plan. By the end of the following season, our ticket revenues had increased by 14 percent, exceeding our $80,000 goal by $4,705. This was the largest amount ever received to date from ticket sales.

The actual number of tickets sold in 2007 did not increase compared with the previous summer. During 2006, sales had already increased, thereby offsetting the 2005 season's loss. With similar attendance figures for 2006 and 2007, it was Joanne's suggestions that enabled us to optimize the potential ticket income for the festival, as well as the Opera House.

By continuing to learn about and to try their new approaches over the years, I became convinced that the TRG staff members are truly the experts on the cutting-edge of keeping many performance industries afloat. Since our encounter with them in 2006 and later, their research and discoveries continue to assist for-profit and nonprofit cultural institutions. They now even have offices in the UK.

Several memorable events had marked the 2006 season. First was the inclusion of the festival in the *New York Times* "Arts and Leisure Summer Stages" feature on Sunday, May 14. In Illinois, the three recommended events were the Grant Park Music Festival, Ravinia Festival, and Woodstock Mozart Festival. Interestingly, young Austrian conductor Christoph Campestrini's second appearance with us occurred just before making his first appearance in the Grant Park concerts.

At our performances, Christoph accompanied two young brothers: violinist Colin Jacobsen and cellist Eric Jacobsen. These three "live wires" lit up the Opera House with Brahms' Double Concerto, undoubtedly inspired by an impromptu pre-weekend celebration at Crystal Lake's 1776 Restaurant. It took place on the restaurant's Thursday Tapas Special evening. As I remember, there were nine tapas courses. Each was served with a different wine, as the proprietor, Andy Andreske, was a wine expert. (He even had his own TV program about wines.) I had fish, salad, coffee, and no wine, but I enjoyed the ever-escalating ebullience created by this trio, as well as the equally ebullient concerts they provided over the following weekend.

Jeffrey Swan was featured during the second weekend of the 2006 season as soloist and conductor in a piano marathon featuring three Mozart concertos. As a brilliant pianist and scholar, as well as an entertaining raconteur, Jeffrey's visit was savored by all.

During the third weekend, Mark Peskanov played and conducted Vivaldi's Concerto for Violin and Cello with recent Rostropovich Competition winning cellist, nineteen-year-old Marie-Elisabeth Hecker. Also on the program were Haydn's D Major Cello Concerto and Mozart's Violin Concerto No. 3, making it a blockbuster weekend.

For the chamber music concert, I had prepared a narrative of "The First Ten Years" of Mozart's life. This was accompanied by interspersed movements of Mozart's chamber works and visuals projected on a screen behind the players.

As if the season was not intense enough, a publicity opportunity occurred with the taping of an Arts Across Illinois program during the final weekend. The program was subsequently aired on Public Television.

During the League of American Orchestras Concert in 2006, I also had made the acquaintance of Istvan Jaray, a Hungarian conductor who became popular with our orchestra players and audience. Our meeting happened in an unusual way.

At the LA Philharmonic concert, I sat at the highest point in the Walt Disney Concert Hall to check out the acoustics. Joanne Rile, a Philadelphia agent, sat next to me, and we hit it off. During our walk back to the hotel, Istvan fell in step next to Joanne, whom he knew, and I immediately recognized his Hungarian accent.

When Joanne introduced us, I mentioned this to him, and we shared memories of our childhood and the songs we sang. Together, we sang these childhood Hungarian tunes on our way back to the hotel. Along the way, Joanne said right in front of Istvan that he was an excellent conductor, and I should hire him, adding that he was not on the roster of musicians she represented.

I asked Istvan for his card, but he didn't have one. So I gave him mine and asked him to contact me. For months I did not hear from him, and eventually somehow, I was able to contact him through his orchestra in Johnstown, Pennsylvania. Clearly, he was modest about following up on my request, but I was finally able to ask him to send me information about himself and his orchestra.

The minute I looked at the first item in the packet he sent, his orchestra's brochure, I knew he would be great for our festival. He was standing in front of the orchestra smiling, with every member of the orchestra also looking at the camera—and smiling. I had never seen anything like it! And that is just how our orchestra responded when they were with him.*

Having escaped from Hungary during the 1956 revolution, Istvan and another music student endured dangerous and difficult circumstances during their trek into Austria. As violinists, they had left their instruments behind, eventually arriving in London without having finished their degrees at the Franz Liszt Academy. In 1957 Istvan auditioned for the Royal Academy of Music. It was willing to accept him but could not provide him with a scholarship.

A few months later however, he was provided a full scholarship at the Royal College of Music in London. After remaining there for two years, he joined the English National Opera. A few years later he applied to a training institute for conductors in London and was asked to delay his application because there

---

* In the photos of most orchestras, the expressions of the players and conductors are usually serious. Of course, all professional musicians take their roles seriously, but they choose their careers because of the joy of making music. The warmth and joy emanating from the expressions of Maestro Jaray and his team was palpable. His unpretentious love of music was evident, something to which I knew our orchestra would respond.

were several Hungarian conductors already holding top positions in London. Later, he was accepted into the conducting program.

Istvan became a student of Sir Adrian Boult and was a freelance violinist with the London Philharmonic and BBC Orchestras. Through these experiences he worked with other legendary conductors of the era: Pierre Monteux, Sir Collin Davis, Antal Doráti, and Carlo Maria Giulini. Later, following his post as a violinist with Canada's Vancouver Symphony, he served on the faculties of the University of Wisconsin and Carnegie Mellon. He became music director of several orchestras and enjoyed guest appearances with important U.S. and European orchestras.

In 2007, Istvan visited the festival for the first time with Russian pianist Olga Vinokur and immediately became one of the orchestra's favorite conductors.

Maestro Istvan Jaray

During 2007, one of Mark's favorite conductors was engaged. This was Robert Bernhardt, whom he considered particularly adept at assisting soloists. At the time, Bob was music director of the Chattanooga Symphony, and we paired him with outstanding young Israeli clarinetist Alexander Fiterstein.

Although German cellist Marie-Elisabeth Hecker had been invited to return, her new European management required that we provide her new visa. This was unexpected, as we had not been required to do this the year before, and it was something we could not afford. As a result, we invited former Rostropovich Competition winner American cellist Wendy Warner, who gave us a terrific performance of Haydn's C Major Cello Concerto. My piano collaboration with Wendy and Mark during the chamber music concert, The Middle Years, was an especially memorable event.

By now, Louise LeCoque's tenure as board president of six years had ended. In her role she had managed not only to establish fiscal stability, but also remarkable cohesiveness throughout the organization. The 2007 season was dedicated to her.

From the 2007 program book:

> *Her style was relaxed but efficient and her judgment was impeccable. Always gracious, she ran no-nonsense meetings that empowered others. Without this kind of leadership, the festival would not be where it is today. Underlying Louise's actions was her reverence for music—placing it at the highest level of importance.*

In January of 2008, Allen Stromberg from nearby Marengo, Illinois, became the festival's new president. That year's season also was marked by an unusual new concert experience.

British conductor Drostan Hall was engaged to develop a program for the second weekend, on August 9th and 10th. While sharing his thoughts about the upcoming program with me, he mentioned "summer . . . summer evening" and suggested the "Incidental Music" to *A Midsummer Night's Dream* by Mendelssohn.

I thought it was a great idea and immediately envisioned an opportunity to present a little theater along with the music.

Because Drostan had a British accent, I suggested he read excerpts from the original Shakespeare play between the seven movements. I felt this would be an authentic and unique enhancement of the work. And indeed, the audience loved it.

By 2008 it was well past the time for us to recognize another important board member, Beth Wester, who had chaired the Chefs' Showcase Brunch for sixteen years. In her honor, a local chef, Rob Macey (who had contributed to the Brunch for many years), did the honors with a trophy he created out of large cooking utensils. It was tricky to get Beth onstage just before the second half of the performance, but we did it. She was indeed surprised and delighted, spontaneously calling the trophy her Oscar. For all her selfless efforts over the years, if anyone deserved an Oscar for chairing so many successful events, Beth was indeed deserving.

Rob Macey presenting Beth Wester with her
"Benefit Chairman Oscar"

Also during 2008, because one of our two $10,000 donors had retired and moved to another state, we lost an important source of revenue on which we had depended since 2001. To our rescue came Bob and Jane Barkei, who had been important supporters for several years. They had moved to the area after retiring to be near their three viola-playing grandchildren. Bob had been vice president of our board for a few years, and he and Jane had assisted with entertaining conductors and artists with beautiful post-concert dinners in their lovely home. As for the grandchildren, all are now full-fledged professionals with successful careers: one in New York and Europe, and two in the Chicago area.

Bob and Jane Barkei with Anita Whalen

Despite this generous replacement of lost revenue, 2008 was also the first year of the economic downturn. It soon became clear that the festival's survival depended on new approaches.

To address the challenges presented by the 2008 economic downturn, I invited exciting young duo-pianists from Bulgaria, Genova & Dimitrov, to kick off the season. In addition to featuring them in performances, I also asked if they would conduct a master class for piano students and teachers. This was an unusual idea, as during my years of piano study and teaching, I had never attended or been involved in a master class for duo pianists—nor had they. But they agreed to do it. For me, organizing and implementing the event and the other activities associated with it turned out to be a major challenge. My hope was that the increased weekend activities would result in increased audience attendance.

Duo-pianists Genova & Dimitrov

Genova & Dimitrov had just swept the international music scene as first prize winners in all the major duo piano competitions. An impressive signature work in their repertoire was the Concerto for Two Pianos and Orchestra in E Major by Felix Mendelssohn. We welcomed the opportunity to present not only this exciting duo, but also this exciting work, which is seldom heard because of its difficulty. We were not disappointed in the resulting performances.

To elicit interest in the master class and associated concerts, I had special flyers made with multiple opportunities: for the Saturday afternoon recital, Sunday master class itself, and Sunday afternoon concert with orchestra. Special packages were designed to make as many events as possible practical for families at reasonable rates. Then I literally "hit the road!"

Having been an active member of the Illinois State Music Teachers Association (ISMTA) for many years before entering the field of orchestra management, I began visiting the monthly meetings of the fourteen chapters of this organization in Northern Illinois. The meetings usually began at 9:00 a.m., and the distances to some of the chapters from my home were up to seventy-five miles.

Because of my former membership, I was allowed to speak at the meetings, where I made the pitch for participation in this unique opening weekend. Several teachers were interested and prepared students for the master class. To this day, I continue to thank and congratulate all the teachers, students, and parents for their extra time, effort, and expense preparing for this amazing learning opportunity. The weekend itself was exhausting but extremely exciting and very well attended.

From then on, artist recitals and master classes became regular features of every festival. For students to have personal coaching and inspiration from such important and accomplished artists is a rare opportunity, and I was thrilled to be able to begin the tradition.

Dutch conductor Arthur Arnold, who was new to our roster, led the orchestra during the second weekend of the 2009 season. Mark Peskanov, with our players as soloists, was featured during the third weekend when we also presented "The Final Years" of Mozart's Life at the Chamber Music concert.

Although ticket sales everywhere had begun to decline, the first and final weekends of our 2009 season had strong sales. As I had hoped, the master class activities helped us expand the audience during the first weekend. As for the third weekend, it is not unusual for artists who appear regularly and are well known to be favored by the audience. This was clearly the case with Mark and our audience, even during these precarious times.

Since I always kept abreast of how other orchestras were faring, I knew that with the economic downturn, general attendance everywhere was down by 36 percent. This happened to be the case with our second weekend that featured a conductor no one knew. Clearly what was happening elsewhere would also happen to us unless special approaches were implemented. Vigilance and creative new performers and performances continued to be critical for our survival.

There was, however, a welcome sign of encouragement from the City of Woodstock in 2009, an annually renewable $2,500 contribution to the festival.

Chapter 6

INTERLUDE

*A**lthough the country and the festival*** were experiencing the strains of the economy, it is important to mention how many businesses contributed to the event. It is also important to keep in mind that 2010 was our twenty-fourth season. Some who had been contributing since the beginning had sold their businesses and/or moved away. But many others were still supporting us for all those years.

These were Austrian Airlines, with a beautiful Viennese holiday, and the Geneva Inn, with an InnClusive Getaway weekend for the seasons' raffles. GNT Limousine provided all transportation for artists to and from airports; Mary Ellen Marunde of Pump House Flowers, and Elizabeth Crisp of Apple Creek Flowers continued donating beautiful arrangements. Many of the restaurants participating in the annual Chefs' Showcase Brunch continued offering their specialties, and many businesses and individuals also contributed items to the event's silent auction.

Although we paid partial or full fare for the following services, those involved exceeded the call of duty to accommodate the festival's needs:

John Scharres, Managing Director of the Opera House, was always as helpful as possible. A multi-talented administrator, he personally participated in building the acoustical shell segments necessary for focusing the sound of the orchestra from the stage into the hall.

John Scharres, Woodstock
Opera House
former Managing Director

Piano technician Mark Foss was available as needed to tune the rental piano from Steinway a few days after its delivery to the Opera House. This occurred a week prior to the performances (so the piano could acclimatize to the environment). He would re-tune it for rehearsals and concerts—and at any time needed.

Greg Dunham and his staff of the accounting firm of Lindgren, Callihan, Van Osdol & Co. (Now Wipfli LLP) were vital to our well-being, with monthly financial services and annual audits.

Graphic designer Steve Salzbrunn of Kreativ Edge was busy all year with our needs and deadlines. His inspired work was actually the "face" of the festival. Believe it or not, Steve's ancestors originally came from Mozart's hometown of Salzburg, Austria.

As fast as Steve had brochures and other mass mailing materials printed, they were delivered to Brenda and Jerry Schiszik of Lett'r Rip Mailing Service, who also provided exemplary assistance.

Richard Peck and his team of RJ Recording and Sound took care of our recording needs in the most professional way. Not only did their technicians come dressed in coat and tie to the performances, but Richard's follow-up attention to detail in the editing and production of our CDs was of the highest quality.

Denise Graff Ponstein, of Indepth Graphics and Printing was greatly appreciated for her ongoing friendship, wisdom, and wonderful personalized service each year of preparing the festival's program books. In fact, because Denise was a respected, well-liked Woodstock native, her efforts on our behalf were invaluable.

Not only was she terrific at putting together the program book, she also helped make sure it was filled with ads of local businesses. To explain: each spring the festival sent notices to businesses offering an advertising opportunity in the program book. But over time we did not hear from some "regulars," who were perhaps "forgetful" or "tardy" with their commitments. However, by the time the program book was finished, just a few days before the festival began, the ads from those concerns were in the book with checks on the way to our post office box. Clearly, it was Denise's "magic" that accomplished this—and I never had to personally contact anyone.

Because my home was an hour and a half drive from Woodstock during festival weekends, I stayed at the local Holiday Inn Express. The staff there was wonderful.

It was Dot Rawlins of the Alexandria House B&B who out-did herself while taking care of the artists. She also voluntarily offered spectacular post-concert dinners at her beautifully dec-orated home during each season, usually in honor of a concert underwriter. Dot had been the owner of a restaurant in Biloxi, Mississippi, for many years, so she was a fabulous cook and a gracious and entertaining hostess.

We were blessed!

⟶

During the fall of 2009, we had begun to look for a grant writer and for a consultant to provide guidance with forging a new direction for the organization. For eighteen years, I had prepared the grant applications for the Illinois Arts Council, the Aptargroup Charitable Foundation, and the City of Woodstock. I was also primarily responsible for bringing in corporate and individual donations. My schedule was so full, I had no time to explore additional foundation opportunities that I believed should be available to us.

In early 2010 we hired Roberta Stewart of Nonprofit Navigators. As a professional grant writer, Roberta was familiar with foundations that might support us, as well as their funding schedules. By mid-July, new grants had been awarded to the festival by the Gaylord & Dorothy Donnelley Foundation and the Chicago Community Trust Arts Work Fund for Organizational Development.

The Arts Work grant had been written for a specific purpose: to hire a consultant to assist with improving board initiatives for developing increased income sources for the festival. For this, in February 2010, we engaged Suzy Peters, of Susan Peters Associates, to lead us through a capacity building program.

Alexandria House B&B Hostess Dot Rawlins

Suzy's proposal included assessments of the community, of the board's organization and structure, and of the development (fundraising) effort. A plan of action was to follow, one that was to include identification of new board members and donors. Committees were established, and members candidly participated in self-assessment exercises. One emerging goal was for board members to engage in more person-to-person activities, such as welcoming patrons at concerts and at post-concert events. Others were to work to bring two new members onto the board who fully understood and agreed to the necessary financial obligation and to actively engage in fundraising.

Suzy made visits to board members' homes to privately gather as much information as possible about their views and abilities. Her personal efforts exceeded our expectations.

Within a short time the decision was made to discontinue the annual Chefs' Showcase Brunch and instead offer a Musical Brunch in April. The purpose of this event was to entice festival enthusiasts to enjoy an afternoon luncheon and musical program and to introduce a new fundraising initiative.

For the musical program, Mark Peskanov came from New York to perform with me and a small group of musicians from the orchestra.

At the end of the concert, a new donor category was introduced: The Encore Circle, for contributors of $1,000 or more. Longtime festival fan Dr. Ewa Radwanska immediately wrote the first check. By the time the festival began in late July, there were a total of twelve new $1,000 donors in addition to those who had already been contributing at that level or above. We were also able to increase board membership by one returning and three new members, for a total of four.

Soon after this event, the current president resigned his position. Treasurer Ed Streit generously agreed to assume the dual role of treasurer and interim president.

The committees continued their charge to come up with new initiatives. Because the festival occurred over three consecutive weekends during the summer, with no concerts throughout the year, it was decided that a quarterly newsletter be sent to patrons to keep the event in their minds and on their calendars.

The Encore Circle was meant not to replace, but instead to augment the Mozart Festival Society, whose base membership requirement had already been raised to $300. Everyone in these groups was invited to the post-concert gala following the final Saturday evening's performance as guests of the board who served as hosts. The galas were now held in the Stage Left Cafe at the Opera House, a lovely facility resulting from a much-needed Opera House expansion.

A positive note to these precarious times emerged when the festival was compared with other arts organizations. Suzy reported that we were down only 7 percent in ticket sales from the previous year (2009), adding that we were "doing fine." She also pointed out that 25 percent of our audience was coming to the festival from Chicago, sixty miles away,

Because the 2009 master class had been such a hit, two were scheduled for 2010. Again, a new concept was introduced when Mark Peskanov coached fourteen student violinists and five cellists as a group in movements from Vivaldi's *Four Seasons*. Returning pianist Jeffrey Swann also agreed to coach five piano students in solo works during his weekend of concerts. These events enabled us to increase attendance once again.

Although we began to receive additional foundation and corporate funding from MacArthur, Centegra and Mercy Health Systems, and Marengo Tool & Die Works, overall, our individual, corporate, and advertising income continued to decline. By the end of the 2010 fiscal year, we had dipped into our reserve funds for three consecutive years; it was clear that we could no longer continue on this path. The economic downturn was still affecting the economy, and us.

By 2010 Mark Peskanov had been our artistic advisor for twelve years. Although it had been a mutually beneficial relationship, in December of 2010 it became clear we could no longer afford the artistic advisory position. Although we asked Mark to continue performing as soloist and conductor at the festival, he declined. This was disappointing not only to us, but also to our audience.

The year 2011 marked the festival's 25th Anniversary Season and the bicentennial commemoration of the birth of composer Franz Liszt—two occasions worthy of celebration . . . and celebrate we did!

German cellist Peter Hörr opened the season as cellist and conductor. Peter had won an Echo Klassik (Europe's Grammy Award) in 2010 as cellist and conductor in a recording with the Hofkapelle Weimar Orchestra. He had also served as a master class technician worldwide and agreed to lead a master class for us. During his session, Peter guided a participating student in a profound transformation of one of Bach's Unaccompanied Suite movements, an enlightening experience for all.

During the season's second weekend, Hungarian conductor Istvan Jaray joined Ukrainian Liszt specialist Mykola Suk in Liszt's Piano Concerto No. 2. What a performance it was! I had heard this concerto many times while growing up, but never had I heard it like this. Also, in the work there is a cello solo which must be played in a particularly expressive way. Our principal cellist, Nazar Dzhuryn, delivered it so beautifully I knew he deserved to be featured with our orchestra as a future soloist.

During the third weekend, Dutch conductor Arthur Arnold returned for his third festival visit. He launched the final weekend of our 25th season with Prokofiev's dynamic and entertaining Classical Symphony. As soloists, violinist Karina Canellakis* and violist Rose Armbrust Griffin** performed Mozart's Sinfonia Concertante for Violin, Viola and Orchestra. These two young ladies (both Juilliard School and Curtis Institute graduates) knew each other from their participation in chamber music at the Chicago area's Midwest Young Artists Conservatory, and their excitement of working together again was evident in their sparkling performance of the Concertante. The program's finale, Beethoven's romantic and fanciful Symphony No. 7, was a fitting gift from the orchestra for our 25th anniversary celebration.

---

* After performing with us, Karina Canellakis attended the Juilliard School's two-year conducting program and is now the chief conductor of the Netherlands Radio Philharmonic. She also is the principal guest conductor of the London Philharmonic and of the Berlin Radio Orchestra.

** Rose Armbrust Griffin is currently a member of the music faculty of Wheaton College in Wheaten, Illinois, and is married with three young daughters. Rose's two older violist brothers, Doyle and Kyle Armbrust, had performed Bach's Brandenburg Concerto No. 6 with the festival in 2009. These three violists, from the same family, are the grandchildren of festival supporters Jane and Robert Barkei.

Beginning with the festival's first master class initiative in 2008, my schedule had become increasingly intense. In addition to organizing these events, I also became responsible for quarterly newsletters and for attending board committee meetings that had been recommended by our consultant Suzy Peters. Pat Kalina, a neighbor I encountered on my daily walks, had recently retired from an office position at a Chicago law firm. Since she seemed interested in continuing some kind of work, I asked if she'd like to assist me on a part-time basis. She was—and thank goodness!

Because Pat had worked in a professional environment, she was very familiar with computers and copy machines. She also was willing to do clerical tasks such as organizing, filing, ordering supplies, etc. Pat was a big help; she was a good sounding board, and over time, she also became a valued friend.

By the fall of 2011, it had been five years since our last review by TRG (Target Research Group Arts) that had enabled us to optimize ticket sales in 2007. I was aware that TRG was recommending new marketing techniques. With the economic downturn, we felt the need to learn about their advances. In the fall of 2011, I flew to TRG's offices in Boulder, Colorado, for an all-day review and plan for adjusting our marketing approach.

This required a retooling process with varying approaches to various groups of potential subscribers and ticket buyers. For example, a new Super Subscriber category was introduced, with special perks. A new plan for repricing the seats in the Opera House was also implemented, and new materials were designed by Steve Salzbrunn with a clever captivating Mozart logo. These were applied to new rack cards for distribution at new locations, as well as information cards, flyers, posters, and e-blasts.

Professionals were already engaged to design our new website, Facebook page, and press releases. We were pleased to be "in step with the times" despite the mounting challenges we hoped to overcome.

The board had expanded in 2010 when Dr. Mark Schiffer returned and Dr. Al Ottens (retired university professor) and his wife, Amy Ottens (retired special ed teacher), joined. In 2011, another new member come on the board: Dr. Maija Mizens, a toxicologist.

In 2011 we also welcomed a new board president, Tom Svoboda, a retired Lt. Col. in the Marine Corps, who had

Pass the Gavel—President Tom Svoboda,
and retiring Interim President Ed Streit

been a board member for three years. Tom had studied violin for about eight years while growing up, and as an adult he piloted planes that flew off aircraft carriers. His background was truly colorful.

With new energy, these members offered innovative ideas for fundraising for 2012. Amy Ottens, a quilter, managed a quilt raffle that garnered $4,500 by the end of the season. With the retirement of the Chefs' Showcase Brunch, it became necessary to launch a new annual fundraising event. This became an Oktoberfest, to be held in the fall, together with Woodstock's Rotary. Planning the event required many meetings and much effort throughout the year for those involved. By now, Dot Rawlins had sold her Woodstock Bed and Breakfast home, but Dr. Mark Schiffer and his lovely wife Isabel began offering beautiful dinner parties and other special events to introduce potential newcomers to the festival and to honor major donors.

Dr. Mark Schiffer, Geraldine Grennan, and Isabel Schiffer

The 2012 season was a hit in all respects. David Schrader, a popular Chicago specialist in early music, returned to open the season as pianist and conductor with two Mozart piano concertos. Since he had an authentically reproduced forte piano (the kind Mozart would have played), I suggested he bring it to perform a concerto during the first half of the program. I also asked him to play another concerto after intermission on a modern instrument so the audience could hear the contrast. With his usual élan and interesting commentary, David created excitement by actually removing parts of the fortepiano during the first half of the program. He then delivered a superb performance which was appreciated by an enthusiastic audience.

David Schrader dissecting his forte piano

During the second weekend of performances, Grammy Award-winning violinists Igor and Vesna Gruppman appeared in a delightful program featuring a variety of repertoire not yet experienced at the festival: works by Bach, Mendelssohn, Grieg, and even the ethereal Adagietto from Mahler's Symphony No. 5, for which we hired a harpist. This was a favored feature, along with the Concerto for Two Violins and String Orchestra by Malcolm Arnold, which had been composed for the Gruppmans, and for which they had been awarded a Grammy.

Oboist Alex Klein and Maestro Arthur Arnold

During the final 2012 weekend, Brazilian oboist Alex Klein was invited to return to the festival. His appearance was a special occasion because everyone knew Alex from his tenure with the Chicago Symphony when we first engaged him in 1997. Unfortunately, just two years after winning a Grammy for his recording of the Richard Strauss Oboe Concerto in 2002, he resigned his position with the CSO due to a physical condition called musician's focal dystonia which interfered with his playing ability.

However, since then Alex had been able to attach something to his oboe that made playing possible again. Conductor Arthur Arnold had been in touch with him over the years, and acting on our behalf, invited Alex to join him in our upcoming concerts on August 11th and 12th. As a result, we were the first in the Chicago area to once again feature Alex in performance.

The Community Room was packed during the pre-concert Conductor/Artist Conversation to hear Arthur and Alex discuss the program. When it was time for questions from the audience, there were no questions, but rather an outpouring of testimonials delivered by those who had loved Alex's playing with the Chicago Symphony and who were thrilled to see and hear him again. This was a poignant experience for everyone.

And what a comeback performance it was! In addition to a memorable rendition of Mozart's Oboe Concerto, Alex played a special encore, "Choro no Capriccio," which he had composed. It was a set of variations on the famous theme of Nicolo Paganini's 24 Caprices—and the audience went wild.

The 2012 season was dedicated to a very special person who had passed away just a few weeks before on July 4th. This was Dr. Roger Benson, who had been a board member for twelve years. As a compassionate doctor and lover of classical music, Roger's mission in life was one for which he was uniquely gifted. He had been a correctional care physician who provided medical care for the inmates at the Cook County Jail and the Milwaukee County Department of Corrections.

Dr. Roger Benson

As the comments in the program's dedication indicated, he was devoted, not only to his family, but also ". . . to everyone he met . . . to all mankind!" Roger's final gifts were donations on behalf of his passing that were designated for the festival. These literally saved us that year.

Chapter 7

FINALE

Roger Benson's parting gift to the festival saved us in 2012 because we had accumulated unexpected expenses during the year. Due to the new marketing approaches, our printing costs had gone up. Our Facebook page and website were unanticipated but necessary additions, and we suddenly became obliged to pay dues to the League of Chicago Theaters and to Dun and Bradstreet.

In addition, because the festival had been a member of the Woodstock Chamber of Commerce, we had also decided to initiate after-hours mixers with programs by small groups of musicians in May to help familiarize Chamber members with our event. Another necessity was engaging a professional photographer to document the festival for public relations, the website, and other social media.

For this we had hired Annamarie Finzel of Finzel Fotos. Annamarie had taken an attractive photograph of the Mozart banner hung from the lantern in front of the Opera House; it was selected by *Symphony Magazine* for their 2013 Summer

Festivals issue. This gave us an opportunity to exhibit the photo and honor Annamarie at the 2013 mixer.

Festival Banner featured in *Symphony Magazine*

But the biggest financial "hit" in the 2012 unexpected expense category was the Federation of Musicians Union dues assessment. Not only were we obligated to pay payroll and work dues at a higher rate than in the past, but for the first time, also pension dues.

Quick thinking for additional funds was necessary, and there was one remaining fundraising approach not yet initiated. That was to seek underwriters for principal orchestra players' chairs. I am not sure where the idea originated, but many orchestras seemed to utilize this opportunity.

It is a fact: audience members who see and hear the orchestra every year develop favored performers. So I contacted a gentleman who had contributed generously to Roger Benson's memorial fund and who was a member of our audience to launch the process.

This was Dr. James G. Haughton, who had been a mentor to Dr. Benson and of course, was moved by his passing.

I called Dr. Haughton and asked if he would kick off the chair sponsorship effort by underwriting the Concert Master's Chair. Although we had a new concert master, Kevin Case, whom he had never seen, Dr. Haughton and his wife, Vivian B. Sodini, agreed. It was delightful to hear Dr. Haughton, an octogenarian, exclaim that he never thought he would be a trend setter at his age!

By the time the festival opened on July 26, we had underwriters not only for the concert master's chair, but also for those of our principal viola, cello, string bass, flute, and bassoon players. Most of these underwriters had already been contributing at the $1,000 level, and they added an increase to that amount to achieve this new undertaking.

The 2013 season opened with conductor Donato Cabrera and pianist Vassily Primakov during the first weekend and ended with Igor and Vesna Gruppman during the final weekend. Both concerts featured traditional repertoire. But during the middle weekend we navigated into new waters.

The orchestra with Pianist Vassily Primikov and Maestro Donato Cabrera

Throughout the industry, it was becoming clearer that classical music was less popular than it had been. There had never been much audience crossover between classical and pops concerts, so many orchestras began offering ways to attract new audiences. Some featured shorter and lighter end-of-workday concerts; others featured popular movies with live orchestral accompaniment. Obviously, we were unable to do this, considering our limited resources and particularly our name, Woodstock *Mozart* Festival.

What we did do was begin to mix some lighter classical works into our programming, and for the same reason, to try to attract new "experimenters" to our live orchestral experience. We began this by engaging classical French saxophonist Daniel Gauthier another European "Echo Klassik" winner.

The first half of the program was dedicated to traditional works, opening with Mozart's Symphony No. 17. This was followed by Haydn's C Major Cello Concerto, brilliantly performed, as I expected, by our own principal cellist Nazar Dzhuryn. But the second half was a complete change from anything we had ever done.

Conductor Igor Gruppman established a reflective mood with the beautiful Intermezzo from Mascagni's *Cavalleria Rusticana*. Then came French composer Jacques Ibert's contrasting "Concertino da camera" for alto saxophone and orchestra, which moved the listening experience into the twentieth century. Introduced by traffic sounds, the first movement continued to surprise, with alternating serene melodic and active rhythmic sections. The soulful second movement eventually ended with animation that elicited an audience reaction never experienced before: a long enthusiastic applause with *hoots and whistle calls*!

There was another surprise reaction from the audience, a positive but appropriately more subdued reaction to the traditional classical Adagietto from Bizet's *L'Arlésienne Suite* No. 1. From then on, audience responses continued to become more enthusiastic. Schulhoff's "Hot Sonate" incorporated a seductive vamp that alternated with animated jazzy sections, and Iturralde's "Pequena Czarda" elicited light applause and vocal expressions of delight throughout Daniel's appropriately schmalzy delivery. The animated czardas ending elicited a torrent of enthusiasm marked by laughter, foot stomping, hoots, and lots of whistle calls, even beyond what we had seen and heard earlier. Clearly, we were in the presence of a new audience who not only liked the music, but also appreciated Daniel Gauthier's magnificent virtuosity. Looking around the hall, we saw many unfamiliar faces.

Another consultant had visited the festival in 2012 to help the board determine a course of action for the future. Committees of board members, volunteers, audience members, and musicians were involved in several meetings.

The primary issue was, of course, the music. From the Artistic Advisory Committee:

> *The team concurred with the consensus of the musicians expressed at the initial meeting, that the festival should maintain its current programming, remembering that the audience likes vibrant pieces such as the Prokofiev that Anita programmed for the last concert. While it's essential to reach out to new audiences, this should not include altering the type of music (e.g., offering "pops" concerts), the location, or the schedule.*

The other major issue during these sessions was succession, finding a replacement for my position upon my retirement. Since my duties involved both the administrative and artistic roles, finding a replacement seemed unlikely. The only solution seemed to be moving to the traditional music director/executive director arrangement. But after deliberation, the issue was deferred.

Concertmaster Kevin Case with Dr. James Haughton and Vivian Sodini

Principal Violist Erin Pipal with Sonia Svoboda

Principal Cellist Nazar Dzhuryn with his wife, Nara Darjaa
(anonymous sponsor not pictured)

Principal String Bassist Charles Grosz with Amy and Dr. Al Ottens

Principal Flutist Robin Fellows with Dr. Ray and Lynn Pensinger

Principal Bassoonist Lori Babinec with Board
President Dr. Maija Mizens and Chuck Mehlman

However, by 2014 we were introduced to a new venue in which to hold a spring fundraising event: the Place de la Musique in Barrington Hills, Illinois. This opulent estate of Marian and Jasper Sanfilippo houses the world's largest collection of restored mechanical instruments, including the world's largest theatre pipe organ. Another building on the premises, the Carousel Pavilion, includes a collection of antique cars, a steam engine, vintage clocks, a restored caboose, and 1890s Pullman passenger car. Most dazzling in this building is the fully operational restored 1890s complete, original European salon carousel.

The Sanfilippos offer these fabulous venues for large events and performances on the stage of the mansion. Since both opportunities suited our needs, we decided to schedule not only the spring fundraising benefit there, but also a few other events. By 2014, we were looking for new ways to increase our audience. As a result, we decided to hold the chamber music concert, a master class, and a Sunday, August 10, orchestral performance at the Place de la Musique.

Benefit Cochair
Dr. Ewa Radwanska with
Dr. Maija Mizens

Dr. Ewa Radwanska had mentioned a young Polish pianist to me who was pursuing his PhD at Northwestern University. I told her about our plans for the spring event at the Place de la Musique and asked if she thought he'd be interested in performing there. She thought it sounded like a wonderful opportunity. As one thing led to another, she became interested in the event itself. She then asked a young Polish attorney who lived in Barrington to assist with organizing the event.

That attorney was Joanna Dobecka-Lembert, former vice consul of Poland and head of the legal department at the Polish

Benefit Cochair
Joanna Dobecka-Lembert

Consulate in Chicago. Not only was Joanna highly regarded and popular in Chicago's Polish community, she was terrific at organizing this kind of function, and, together with Dr. Radwanska, very effective at bringing in a crowd.

Titled "Be Amazed," it was a grand event, and everyone loved it. When guests entered, they toured the mansion, after which our concert master, Kevin Case, joined pianist Igor Lipinski in a short musical program. The beautiful concert hall, bedecked with magnificent chandeliers from turn-of-the-century theaters, was spellbinding. Afterward, everyone made their way to the Carousel Pavilion where they admired the vintage artifacts. To everyone's delight, the evening's finale was a ride on the French carousel.

The financial results from this undertaking were significant and a tribute to the extensive efforts of Joanna and Dr. Radwanska. To this day I remain deeply grateful to them.

Dr. Judysharon Buck on Carousel ride

With Roberta Stewart's retirement, a new grant writer had come on board in the fall of 2013, Alexandra Nelson of Juno Consulting. Alexandra was an effective addition to our team. She maintained our current foundation support and increased it with gifts from the NIB and Dr. Scholl foundations, as well as from the Arts Work Fund of the Chicago Community Trust. Her association also provided another link in my personal connection to the Stravinskys when she announced during one of our conversations: "I know the Stravinskys!"*

---

* As mentioned in Chapter 1, Igor Stravinsky's son, Soulima Stravinsky, was my piano teacher at the University of Illinois. Alexandra Nelson's father was a professor at the University, and Soulima's wife, Françoise Stravinsky, was Alexandra's French teacher at the University High School.

Françoise Stravinsky sometimes invited her small class of students to the Stravinsky home to practice conversational French and enjoy baked treats and a musicale by Soulima. At the time, none of the students made the family connection. They just thought Soulima was a terrific piano player!

At the ceremony to accept a color printer from the Arts Work Fund, another recipient of a grant from the Arts Work Fund, Valerie Moore, introduced herself to me. Valerie had recently completed a master's degree in arts administration, and because she also had an undergraduate degree in viola, she was interested in the festival.

Although we did not have a position on our staff for her, I was excited to meet her. I knew that because of her recent education she would be familiar with the latest technology for not-for-profit work. We still needed, but had not been able to begin to develop, a database. As expected, Valerie knew what to do. Within a short time we signed a contract for her to begin the project on an hourly basis. This was another example of the festival's serendipity: meeting someone who had the skills the festival needed.

During the first weekend of the 2014 season, clarinetist Alexander Fiterstein and conductor Istvan Jaray returned to the festival at the Woodstock Opera House with wonderful performances of the Overture to Rossini's *The Italian Girl in Algiers,* Mozart's Clarinet Concerto and Haydn's *Clock* Symphony. At my request, in honor of his Israeli heritage, Alex performed a special Klezmer encore, "Sirba Tarras," arranged for string orchestra by Alexander Zhurbin.

For the chamber music concert at the Place de la Musique, Igor Lipinski and Alex Fiterstein were joined by our players in Mozart's Piano Quartet, K. 478 and his Clarinet Quintet. Following the concert, Alex led an inspired master class for clarinet students.

During the second weekend, pianist Igor Lipinski was accompanied by Maestro Jaray in Mozart's Piano Concerto No. 7. Also on the program were Mendelssohn's "Hebrides Overture" and Mozart's *Linz* Symphony. These concerts were again held at the Woodstock Opera House and attended by many Polish patrons who had attended the spring benefit.

The performances of the final weekend again featured Igor and Vesna Gruppman. The Saturday evening concert was at the Woodstock Opera House, and the Sunday performance at the Place de la Musique. Because we had had such a positive response the previous year to saxophonist Daniel Gauthier by an enthusiastic "new" audience, we asked Igor Gruppman to design a concert on the lighter side. We hoped this would entice some of the new audience members to return to the Saturday evening performance at the Woodstock Opera House, or out of curiosity, to the Place de la Musique the next day. We also knew that other concerts at the Place de la Musique were generally on the lighter side, and we hoped that many of their patrons would attend our performance.

The first half of the program included Mozart's *Eine kleine Nachtmusik*, "Winter" from Vivaldi's *Four Seasons*, and a Vivaldi Concerto for Two Violins. The second half featured Warlock's *Capriol Suite for Strings*, Piazzolla's familiar "Tango Oblivion," and a special arrangement of two movements of Piazzola's *The Four Seasons of Buenos Aires*.

The audiences' responses to these concerts were enthusiastic. It was clear, however, that the newcomers who had attended the saxophone concert the previous year had not returned, as these selections were clearly not in the same genre that had attracted them the year before.

Still determined to continue to spread the word of the festival and attract new audiences, in the spring of 2014 we also scheduled short chamber music concerts in outlying areas. For these we featured our new Woodstock Mozart Festival String Trio, comprised of concert master Kevin Case, violist Elizabeth Hagen, and principal cellist Nazar Dzhuryn. An evening concert was held at nearby Sun City, in Huntley, and a Sunday afternoon concert at the Cuneo Mansion, in Vernon Hills.

The Board of Directors elected Dr. Maija Mizens as a new president at the Annual Meeting in 2013. Extremely enthusiastic about the festival, Maija was an informed lover of classical music. She and her husband, Chuck, had come to the area from Cleveland, and during their visits to family back home, they continued attending Cleveland Orchestra performances.

Maija approached whatever needed to be done with intelligence, wisdom, and energy. Since joining the board she had actively participated in festival activities, making solicitation calls, volunteering at events and working on the Oktoberfest.

Woodstock's Rotary generously agreed to work with us on the Oktoberfest as their Public Service Project, and the first event was held in a tent on September 6, 2012. Unfortunately, it was a cold night, and attendance was low. The financial results were disappointing, but all expenses were covered. The committee realized that since it was a first-time attempt, it might take a few years for the event to get off the ground, and they planned to try again the following year, 2013.

Optimistically hoping for better weather, they decided to expand the event to two days: Friday night and Saturday afternoon, September 13 and 14, 2013. Although attendance was limited on Friday evening because of rain, the next day was beautiful. The atmosphere was delightful with music from Die Musicmeisters and Sun City Huntley's Let's Dance Band.* A larger tent accommodated a substantially larger crowd, and the beautiful weather, aroma from the grills, animated beer drinking contests, and family activities on the lawn made for a great time.

However, it rained on the Friday evening of the next Oktoberfest in 2014, again resulting in limited attendance. Although the weather improved on Saturday, the event resulted in a financial loss. Rotary generously covered the shortfall, but obviously the Oktoberfest would not be continued in 2015.

The success of the spring benefit at the Place de la Musique in 2014 encouraged the board to hold another "Be Amazed!" benefit at that venue in April 2015. With an example to follow from the previous year, they planned and hosted a wonderful event. Invitations were sent to our patrons and several groups, including repeat invitations for many from the Polish crowd. There was an auction and a raffle. David Schrader, a fine keyboard artist and gifted raconteur, presented an entertaining—as well as musically and technically impressive—organ recital in the beautiful concert hall.

The crowd was not as big as the year before, resulting in a more modest financial outcome; however, all who attended had a wonderful time.

___

* Maija Mizen's husband, Chuck Mehlman (an outstanding amateur trumpet player), played in Sun City's Let's Dance Band and arranged for the group to perform at the Oktoberfest, prompting many couples to enjoy dancing as well.

The board began strategic planning after the 2015 benefit. Activities for producing the coming season were also underway. In 2015 performances were again divided between the Woodstock Opera House and the Place de la Musique.

Pianist Mykola Suk agreed to play on two of the weekends. During the opening weekend at the Opera House, he was joined by concert master Kevin Case and principal cellist Nazar Dzhuryn in Beethoven's Triple Concerto, with Brian Groner conducting. During the second weekend, Igor and Vesna Gruppman appeared at the Place de la Musique with another varied, lighter program that included works by Bach, Vivaldi, Holst (*St. Paul Suite*), and "Summer" and "Autumn" from Piazzolla's *Four Seasons of Buenos Aires*. The program ended with a beautiful arrangement of "Smoke Gets in Your Eyes" for violin and orchestra by Jerome Kern.

Vesna and Igor Gruppman at the Place de la Musique

During the morning on Friday, Vesna rehearsed with her viola. But a special undertaking was necessary for the afternoon rehearsal when she needed her violin. This required a quick trip to Chicago's O'Hare International Airport to intercept her Guadagnini violin between rehearsals. Because her violin had been on loan to a former student in San Diego, the student was flying to Chicago to return the violin.

Vesna's former student left San Diego on Friday morning, July 31st. I was to meet him at the airport when he arrived in Chicago and take the violin to Vesna before the afternoon rehearsal, which began at two o'clock. Reluctant to shoulder this responsibility alone, I asked Tetsuo Matsuda, a fine violin maker who lives near the Place de la Musique, to go with me.

He drove and generously brought along one of his violins to lend to the former student for a month. The instrument exchange was accomplished in minutes on the lower concourse of the O'Hare terminal; the former student caught the next flight back to San Diego, and we delivered the Guadagnini to Vesna just before the rehearsal began. For me, this was a stressful experience. For Tetsuo, who is used to these matters, it was business as usual.

During the final weekend of performances at the Opera House, pianist Mykola Suk was joined by Igor Gruppman as conductor for Beethoven's Piano Concerto No. 5 (Emperor). Mozart's Divertimento in D Major, K. 136 and his Symphony No. 40 completed the program.

Suk and Gruppman's New York agent, Erica Shupp, had been saying for years how special their collaboration was with this piano concerto. I believed her because she had sent me several wonderful artists. Also, this was the year I would be able to make good use of Mykola's talent in two orchestra concerts, as well as in a piano recital.

The results were amazing. My doctor was in the audience attending the festival for the first time. He was so impressed with the concert he told me at intermission that in the future, he was going to come to *all* of our concerts. What a finale for the 2015 season.

Continuing with our attempt to attract new audiences, we presented three outreach string trio concerts of "The First Ten Years" of Mozart's life program. These were held at McHenry County College, Aurora University, and the Unitarian Church in Naperville.

Also, during 2015, I had been planning ahead for the 2016 season, although by this time we were planning for only two concerts due to our dwindling resources. For one of these, we invited conductor Istvan Jaray to return with duo-pianists Lavrova and Primakov.

Our son Chuck, who was employed by Merck Pharmaceuticals, was at a management conference in Florida early in the fall. At one of the sessions, an orchestra was featured with conductor Roger Nierenberg in a program titled "The Music Paradigm."

Roger had developed a unique presentation of leadership approaches for business personnel gatherings. On the podium in front of the orchestra, he demonstrated different leadership styles that could easily be interpreted in any industry or business: over gesticulating to the orchestra players is the equivalent of micromanaging; instructing the orchestra to just watch him, then doing little is an example of a leaderless style. Other approaches were demonstrated as well, and after each, Maestro Nierenberg circulated with a microphone among the players, asking about their reactions. In response to the ineffective styles, players expressed their frustrations or annoyances. If the styles were easy to follow and helpful, their comments were positive.

Chuck called to tell me about the session and sent me a short video he'd taken while seated behind the orchestra. A musician himself, he was thrilled with the experience, thinking this might be something I would be interested in for Woodstock. In fact, I was very interested.

I could envision an opportunity to involve the business community in McHenry County to attend a session along these same lines with Roger, then feature him in a concert in 2016. Several testimonials by those who had attended his sessions were posted on the Music Paradigm website. Among them were comments from participants who had never attended a live orchestra concert but who were so moved by the experience they planned to do so in the future.

I called Roger's agent, Edna Landau, to see if engaging Roger would be possible. After a few weeks, she returned my call and said he'd agreed to come to Woodstock. In fact, he was to be in St. Charles, Illinois, soon and would like to meet with me and see the Opera House. We met, he saw the Opera House, and I arranged details of the second summer performance with Edna.

A special experience connected with my association with Edna Landau is worth mentioning. When she called to tell me of Roger's agreement to perform with us, she began by saying she owed me an apology. I did not know what the apology could be about since she had been very agreeable during our first call. She then apologized for not having heard of the Woodstock Mozart Festival. I said I did not blame her; it was a small festival in an out-of-the-way place.

She added that she had recently run into Henry Fogel at a conference in New York. Some may remember Henry as the former president of the Chicago Symphony with whom I had interviewed for a job years before. She said she asked Henry about the Woodstock Mozart Festival, specifically, "How is it?" Edna said he answered, "It's wonderful."

⁓

As reports from the 2015 season emerged, it became clear that moving ahead with a 2016 season was uncertain. Although the attendance at the Opera House had increased somewhat in 2015, attendance at the Saturday performance at the Place de la Musique concerts had not materialized as anticipated.

By October, although our bills were being paid, checking on promised donations and forthcoming bills had become a daily exercise. We received notice that our MacArthur Fund for Arts and Culture grant would not be renewed due to the foundation's decision to fund only Chicago-based organizations.

There was also discussion regarding how to further curtail spending, as the budget for 2016 already projected a $4,000 loss. One suggestion was from board member Marcia Koenen, Director of the Aurora University Woodstock Center, who offered to take over maintenance of the database.

From the November 19th board meeting minutes:

> *Mizens and Buck discussed the perils of continuing, as the deficit after the 2015 season would likely be larger next year. Whalen pointed out that closing the festival would entail hiring a lawyer to file a document. We owe our Director $13,000, of which at least $4,000 must be paid according to*

our last audit. Al Ottens said that the prudent thing would
be to wind up.

Although board meetings were not usually scheduled in
December, the board decided to convene on December 15, 2015.
It was clear that by the end of November our bank balance was
at a historic low, and it was also clear that we would not have
the amount needed to start the new year. No one wanted to go
deeper into debt, and everyone acknowledged that new fundraising efforts would be impossible to launch. Another critical
point was that we had been losing money for about ten years.

From the December 15th, 2015, board meeting minutes:

Al Ottens made a motion to begin the process of dissolving
the charter of the organization and begin working to elim-
inate the debt. After additional discussion of fundraising
efforts, including suggestions by new board member Paul
Skowronski, Schiffer seconded the motion to dissolve. The vote
on the motion to dissolve was 6 AYE and 3 AGAINST. The
motion carried. Al Ottens moved that the board members
and spouses need a celebration of the achievements of the
festival to go out on a high note. All agreed.

Al Ottens wrote the following message, which was posted
on our website:

To Our Community of Supporters:
It is with great regret that we announce that the Woodstock
Mozart Festival will close after this past season, our 29th.
All of us associated with the Festival—musicians, Board

members, Director—extend our deep appreciation to all who have attended concerts and contributed to make the Festival such a value to the Woodstock community—and beyond. We will miss performing for you . . .

Postlude

Not long ago, I thought about an occasion during my middle school years that seemed connected to the career I never anticipated in arts management. I remembered my fascination with the Russian impresario Sol Hurok whose life was depicted in the movie *Tonight We Sing*. While I was growing up, his name had been mentioned, along with those of the artists my parents talked about. I came to know that he was responsible for bringing many of them to America, among them: ballerina Anna Pavlova, violinist David Oistrakh, pianists Emil Gilels and Sviatoslav Richter, and cellist Mstislav Rostropovich. He also managed Artur Rubinstein, Marian Anderson, Van Cliburn, Jan Peerce, and many others.

I so vividly remember attending the movie because when I walked out of the theater, I thought, "That is the neatest job anyone could have!" As a result, I cannot help but think of this as a prophetic moment in my life.

I know I am not alone in having had this kind of realization. I remember Maestra Catherine Comet telling me about a similar experience she had when only three years old. Her mother had taken her to an orchestral performance in Paris, and when they came out from the concert, Catherine told her mother that when she grew up she wanted to do what the man in front of the orchestra did. At the time, I doubt there were any female conductors, but as we know, Catherine became one of the first. And we were lucky to feature her in Woodstock.

Fast forward to May 1992. The *Naperville Sun* newspaper asked to interview me about my new post as Executive Director of the Woodstock Mozart Festival. In the fall of 2019, it was interesting for me to reread my interview remarks from this article while preparing to write this account of my journey.

"I don't view classical music as an elitist discipline. I think it is a tremendous inspiration to humanity. That's why I am willing to work very hard for it. The higher the performance level, the more inspired we can become. It creates a reaction in people of excitement, a passion that will reach anybody, even young children."

Clearly, as it had done for me!

"There is a tremendous spiritual attraction if music is presented in the way it was intended. I'm always interested in education and working toward helping people to appreciate higher standards."

It is said that the person in charge of a project should have a vision. Having never thought consciously until much later about this, reviewing the remarks I had made in this article years earlier struck a chord. I suppose this was my vision for what I hoped the Woodstock Mozart Festival would become.

We all know the adage "Birds of a feather flock together." My view is more like: "The vibration one emanates attracts those who are like-minded." Or, "What we put out comes back to us." Or, "What goes around comes around." While writing about my journey, I came to appreciate that those who joined in developing the festival clearly were "birds of a feather," and that this is what enabled us to achieve together the level of performance we envisioned.

My deepest appreciation goes to all those mentioned in this writing, beginning with my parents, who provided such a rich cultural background of experiences throughout my life until they passed away. I must say I felt very reassured when, at age ninety (2002), my mother put her stamp of approval on the festival. I have come to realize that what I learned from them can never be learned in a classroom. Of course, what I learned from my many teachers and mentors completed what was also critical for me to be able to achieve my goal.

Charlie Whalen and Jim Wester

Most of all, I thank my husband, Charlie, for the enormous amount of time and expertise he was willing to invest in what became our joint project together. His professional expertise as a lawyer was invaluable, as were his excellent writing skills. He willingly looked over letters, and particularly legal and business-related documents I casually deposited on the kitchen table for his review. His suggestions about dealing with all facets, including board and community relations, were invaluable. Without him, the festival would not have achieved what I had envisioned for it.

In 1994, two years after I joined the organization, Linda Ender described the festival as a "phoenix rising from the ashes." In 2002, the then former board president, Dr. Ray Pensinger, wrote that "I too, have to pinch myself from time to time about our good fortune in having a topflight organization from top to bottom." In 2009, patron Barbara Tryon Andreas commented in a letter: "Last evening all in attendance let you and your accompanying musicians know just how much your performance was appreciated, the stand-up applause of great duration intended to demonstrate to all you musicians the magical musical spiritual energy you had conveyed to all of us!!"

Conversation ensues following such a concert as the crowd slowly moves down the steps to the ground floor. . . . There is no talk about the issues of the day or the tough times we are in. Rather: "I'm so thrilled . . . I'm from Highland Park . . . Antioch . . . Zion, Wisconsin . . . I'm so pumped up, It was glorious," and on and on. . . . "See you next year!"

After 2015, there was no next year, which, considering the effects of the COVID-19 pandemic, is just as well. For those who had been involved, former president Louise LeCoque wrote, "We have wonderful memories that we shall always treasure. It was a great ride!!"

I mentioned in my final remarks to the board in 2016 at our Turn Out the Lights party: "As we remember our final season, I know we agree that it was worth the effort to continue (probably two years longer than we might have), so we could go out as we did . . . shall we say, on a rocket!"

With deepest gratitude, my assessment of all that happened throughout my life in preparation for my mission in music applies to everyone's personal mission. May I suggest, "If you don't believe in God's plan (for you) just take a look at what you have experienced."

Anecdotes

1995 This year marked Mark Peskanov's first visit to the festival. Because he lived in New York City, he was quite enamored of seeing the farmland around Woodstock. As we drove around, he wanted all the windows down in the car. He loved the breeze blowing through with the smell of fresh-mowed grass and sat in the back seat offering to play any selections I would like to hear. I only remember two selections that I requested: Sarasate's "Zigeunerweisen" and Mendelssohn's Violin Concerto. He knocked these out (actually, just excerpts from the concerto), and others I requested. At the time, I thought this was quite amazing—and I still do.

1997 Daniel Gaisford was the cello soloist in 1997. He had decided to drive to Woodstock from his parents' home in Utah with his cute little dog. None of the motels in town allowed pets, and as a result, he ended up staying in his RV at a nearby campgrounds. During rehearsals and the concert, Daniel wanted the dog to stay in the dressing room, which was on the floor above the stage. I objected, but he insisted the dog would be well behaved . . . that he was house trained and would not bark. In both cases, these promises turned out to be false.

1999 During the festival, Mark and I stayed at the Holiday Inn Express in Woodstock in rooms that overlooked a lovely park-like area. One morning, my phone rang at 7:00 a.m. when I was not yet awake. It was Mark, excitedly telling me to look out the window at the bunny in this park area. To Mark, who lived in Manhattan, seeing a live bunny was a novelty. To me, with a home and yard in the suburbs, seeing a bunny was a regular occurrence that often became an annoyance when the bunny ate our plants.

1999 French hornist Otto Carrillo played with us that summer. During the festival he received a call from Chicago's Grant Park Music Festival offering him a position in their orchestra. That festival was much more high profile than the Woodstock Mozart Festival, and the pay was more generous.

Later I heard that Otto had turned down the Grant Park orchestra offer, saying that he was having too good a time in Woodstock. Before our season ended, Otto was offered a position in the Chicago Symphony horn section, where he remains to this day.

2004 During the first weekend of this season, we featured The Vienna Piano Trio in Beethoven's Triple Concerto. When the musicians arrived, they were particularly excited to be in Woodstock because it had been the setting of one of their favorite movies, *Groundhog Day*! Having become aware of this, B&B proprietor Dot Rawlins rented the movie for them to watch during their visit.

2004 During the second weekend of the 2004 season, Hungarian conductor Gregory Vajda led the orchestra when Italian pianist

Roberto Prosseda was the soloist in Mozart's Piano Concerto No. 27. Because the Opera House was open from 9:00 a.m. to 5:00 p.m., it was a challenge for pianists to use the piano to practice, since orchestra rehearsals occupied most of the day. Therefore, Roberto could use the piano only from 9:00 a.m. until 10:00 a.m., when orchestra rehearsal began, and then at 12:30 p.m. during the lunch hour for an hour and a half.

As a result, just after the morning orchestra rehearsal ended at 12:30 p.m. on Friday, Roberto went to practice the piano, expecting to continue until the two o'clock rehearsal, when his participation was scheduled. At half past twelve I left the hall with the conductor for lunch. When we got to the park in front of the Opera House, Roberto came running out to us, quite upset. The Opera House played CDs from previous festival performances on the intercom in the park during the lunch hour each day. Roberto could hear what was being played while inside the Opera House as well. Unbelievably, it was the same concerto he was practicing, which had been performed during a previous season by another artist. Poor Roberto was confused, thinking somehow his rehearsal had already begun! Of course, we informed him otherwise, and he returned to the hall to practice.

2004 It also happened that Roberto Prosseda played a custom-built, Italian Fazioli piano. Since a local piano vendor in Chicago carried the Fazioli line, one of his pianos was provided at no cost to us for Roberto's weekend at the festival. In return, we were obliged to promote the Fazioli instrument in our program book and from the stage.

Betty Thomas Stork was the board member who was to welcome the audience from the stage that weekend. As a florist, Betty had never heard of this kind of piano and asked me why it was so special. I explained that in the piano world, a Fazioli instrument could be compared to a Maserati car in the automobile world. As she played around with these two Italian words, I became concerned. Sometimes, those who welcomed the audience from the stage became distracted by the stage lights and the audience. Because of this, they occasionally faltered with what they had intended to say. I hoped the piano would not be identified as a Maserati. Luckily, Betty did just fine.

2006 See Symphony–Section 3 I've already described the exuberant opening weekend of the 2006 season with conductor Christoph Campestrini, violinist Colin Jacobsen, and cellist Eric Jacobsen, which began with a nine-course tapas dinner (page 78). As usual, after the Saturday night performance, a celebratory party was held.

It is important to mention that all three young men were quite handsome, but only the conductor was married. Having extended my compliments to Eric for a wonderful performance, I asked him if he had met the "right" girl yet, meaning the one he hoped to marry. His answer: "Oh yes . . . many times!"

2013 Igor and Vesna Gruppman had first visited the festival as guest artists in 2012. By 2013, we had gotten to know each other quite well. Also, by then I had considered trying a performance at the Place de la Musique for the first time in 2014. Since the Gruppmans were popular with our audience, I was sure they would be returning in 2014. I asked them to go with me to look at the new location. I was interested in their opinion as performers about how suitable they felt the venue would be.

I had a difficult time getting them to find a few hours to make the trip. We were ready to go when an old friend from Milwaukee unexpectedly stopped by the Opera House to see them after a rehearsal. This delayed matters further. Finally, I was able to take them to the Place. Once there, I could not get them out the door to go to the studio of nearby violin maker Tetsuo Matsuda, who was expecting us. They were so fascinated by the artifacts, mechanical instruments, and opulent decor that they did not want to leave. They also thought the Place was a fabulous performance venue.

When we arrived at Mr. Matsuda's studio, a marathon ensued as the Gruppmans tried out many violins and violas. It was like seeing two kids in a candy shop. Eventually, this marathon ended at the intervention of Mrs. Matsuda, who suggested we all go for dinner at a nearby restaurant.

2013 After finishing his rehearsal for the benefit at the Place de la Musique, Polish pianist Igor Lipinski and I listened to some piano rolls by famous artists. The one that surprised us both was Artur Rubinstein's obvious embellishment of a Chopin waltz with something we knew was not in the score.

Anita Whalen

About the Author

In 1988 *Anita Whalen* was drafted into orchestra management by the Fox River Valley Symphony in Aurora, Illinois. Four years later, she began a distinguished twenty-four-year career as Artistic and General Director of Illinois' Woodstock Mozart Festival, overseeing every aspect of the annual three-weekend summer event. She expanded the repertoire beyond Mozart to notable composers including Bach, Vivaldi, Haydn, Beethoven, Mendelssohn, Prokofiev and others, attracted world-class soloists, and added fresh new programs that made the festival a much-loved destination for exceptional classical music.

Whalen studied at the University of Illinois as a piano performance major with Soulima Stravinsky, son of Igor Stravinsky. She later become a piano teacher, a teaching consultant, and founder/director of a school of piano instruction before entering the field of arts management. Retired since 2016, Whalen and her husband, Charles, live in Naperville, Illinois, their home for more than fifty years.

Index

###
1776 Restaurant, 78

A
A. Sulka and Company, 2
Aiken, Michael, 37
Alexandria House B&B, 92
AMADEUS HARMONIE wind
      octet, 69–70
Amcore Foundation, 46
analytics in marketing, 76–78
Anders, Mariedi, 56
Apple Creek Flowers, 49, 89
Aptargroup, Inc., 46, 63
Armbrust, Doyle, 97n
Armbrust, Kyle, 97n
Arnold, Arthur, 87, 97, *102,*
      102–103
Arrau, Claudio, 9
Artistic Advisory Committee on
      programming changes, 109
Arts Across Illinois, 79

arts administrator position, 18–24
"Arts and Leisure Summer Stages,"
      New York Times, 78
audience reaction to lighter pro-
      gramming, 108–109
Austrian Airlines, 89
Austrian Airlines raffle, 49

B
Babinec, Lori, *44–45,* 68, *112*
Baird, Audrey, 20
Balter, Alan, 38, 41, 43, 53
Barge Music, 59
Barkei, Bob, *84*
Barkei, Jane, *84*
Baton Rouge Symphony, 9, 48,
      60
Bauer, Harold, 17
Bauer, Sally, 17
Beacraft, Ross, 34, 37, 40
Beethoven
      Piano Concerto No. 5, 121

12 Variations on a Theme from *The Magic Flute*, 55

Symphony No. 7, 97

Triple Concerto,120

Benson, Roger, *103*

Bernhardt, Robert, 81

Bicket, Harry, 61

Bing, Rudolph, 17

Black, Ralph, 22–24, *23*

Blazier, Bob, 63

Board of Directors

   closing of festival, 125–126

   mission statement, 57

   Mizens, Maija, 99, 118

   motion to dissolve charter, 125–126

   resignations and replacements, 33–34

   Streit, Ed, 66

   Wester, Beth, 35

   Whalen's hiring, 26–28

   Zanck, Charie, 45–46

Brahms, Double Concerto, 78

Bremner, Belinda, x

Buck, Judysharon, *115*, 124

Bullen, Sarah, 61

business community involvement, 123

Busse Thomas Flowers and Gifts, 49

C

Cabrera, Donato, 107, *107*

caféhaus musik, 62

Cahill, Catherine, 38

Campbell, Daniel, *73,* 73–74

Campestrani, Christoph, 78, 136

Canellakis, Karina, 97

Carillo, Otto, 134

Carousel Pavilion (Place de la Musique), 113, 114, *115*

Case, Kevin, *110,* 120

Caufield, Clarice, 63, *65*

Caufield, Farlin, 63, *65*

Chefs' Showcase Brunch, 35, *36,* 46, 63, 94

Chicago Community Trust Arts Work Fund for Organizational Development, 92

Chicago Symphony, ix, 9, 12, 25–26, 51–53, 61, 124, 134

Chicago Tribune, 26, 38, 61, 76

Comet, Catherine, 36–37, 40, *47,* 51–52, 127

Concert Master Chair underwriting, 107

Conductor/Artist Conversations, 51–52

Cooper, Emil, 10

Craine's Chicago Business, 40

Crisp, Elizabeth, 89

Cugat, Xavier, 2

D

Darjaa, Nara, *111*

Davis, Collin, 81

Dickens, Jake, ix
Die Musicmeisters, 119
Dobecka-Lembert, Joanna, 114, *114*
Donath, Helen, 67
Donath, Klaus, 67
Doráti, Antal, 81
Dunham, Greg, 90
Dzhuryn, Nazar, 97, 108, *111,* 120

E
Eastman School of Music audition, 12
Elgin Symphony, 34, 43–44
Encore Circle, 94–95
Ender, Jon, 46, 54, 66, *66*
Ender, Linda, 46, 66, *66*

F
Fellows, Robin, *112*
Ferru, Frank, *36*
"The Final Years" of Mozart's Life, 87
Finzel, Annamarie, 105
Finzel Fotos, 105
"The First Ten Years" of Mozart's life, 79
  outreach projects, 122
Fiterstein, Alexander, 81, 116
Fodor, Eugene, 36
Fogel, Henry, 25, 124

Fokine, Michael, 2
Foss, Mark, 90

G
Gaisford, Daniel, 53, 54, 133
Gauthier, Daniel, 108–109
Gaylord & Dorothy Donnelley Foundation, 92
Geneva Inn, 49, 89
Genova & Dimitrov, *85,* 85–86
Giulini, Carlo Maria, 81
GNT Limousine, 89
Graf, Hans, 55–56, *65*
Grant Park Music Festival, 78
Grennan, Geraldine, 66, *67, 100*
Griffin, Rose Armbrust, 97
Groner, Brian, 120
Grosz, Charles, *111*
Gruppman, Igor, 101–102, 107–108, 117, 120, *120*, 121, 136
Gruppman, Vesna, 101–102, 107, 117, 120, *120*, 121, 136

H
Hall, Drostan, 82–83
Harris, Russell, 67
Haughton, James G., 107, *110*
Haydn
  C Major Cello Concerto 54, 82, 108
  D Major Cello Concerto, 79

Clock Symphony, 116
Hecker, Marie-Elisabeth, 79
Heifetz, Jascha, 2
Herzog, Helen. *See* Zell, Helen
    (Herzog)
Hindemith, Paul, 16
Hofkapelle Weimar Orchestra, 96
Hollywood Bowl, 2
Hörr, Peter, 96
Hummel, Johann Nepomuk, 37n
    Trumpet Concerto, 37
Hungarian Little Theatre, 2–3
Hurok, Sol, 127

I
Illinois Arts Council, 26–32, 92
ISMTA (Illinois State Music Teachers
    Association), 16–17, 86

J
Jacobsen, Colin, 78, 136
Jacobsen, Eric, 78, 136
Jaray, Istvan, 79–81, *81,* 96, 116
Jones Beach, 5
Jupiter Symphony, 54

K
Kalina, Pat, 98
Kanzia, Karen, 49
Keleher, Lila, 71–72, *72*
Kern, Jerome, 120
Kim, Chun-Myung, 40

Klein, Alex, 53, 102, *102*
Knott's Berry Farm, 2
Koenen, Marcia, 124
Kraehenbuehl, David, 16
Kreativ Edge, 90

L
La Bohème Met broadcasts on
    Saturdays, 5
Labella, Peter, 11
Lagios, Maria, 36
Landau, Edna, 123
leadership approaches, "The
    Music Paradigm," 122–123
League of American Orchestras,
    20–22, 24, 34, 76, 79
LeCoque, Erv, 62–63, *65*
LeCoque, Louise, 62–63, *65,* 82, 130
Les Sylphides ballet music, 2
Let's Dance Band, 119
Levine, Robert, 53
Lindgren, Callihan, VanOsdol
    & Co., 90
Lipinski, Igor, 116, 137
Liszt, bicentennial commemora-
    tion and, 96–97
Loebel, David, 54

M
Macey, Rob, 83
Mahler
    "Adagietto", 102

Marunde, Mary Ellen, 89
master classes, 86–87, 95–96
  Genova & Dimitrov, 85
Matsuda, Tetsuo, 121, 137
Medford, Gene, 54
Mehlman, Chuck, *112,* 119n
Mendelssohn
  A Midsummer Night's Dream
    "Incidental Music", 82
  Concerto for String Orchestra,
    55
  Concerto for Two Pianos, 86
  Hebrides Overture, 117
  Octet in E flat, 55
Menuhin, Jeremy, 70–71
Menuhin, Yahudi, 70–71
Mesta, Perle, 48–49
Met broadcasts on Saturdays, 5
Milwaukee Symphony, 33, 44
Mizens, Maija, 99, *112, 113,*
  124–126
  Board of Directors election, 118
Molthen, John, 49
Monteux, Pierre, 81
Moore, Dennis, 39
Moore, Valerie, 116
Moser, Barbara, 41
Mozart
  Clarinet Quintet and Concerto,
    60
  Concerto for Two Pianos with
    Boogie Woogie encore, 67

Dances and Marches, 55
Divertimento, K. 136, 121
Eine kleine Nachtmusik, 117,
  140
"Exultate, Jubilate," 67
Gran Partita Serenade, 41–43
Horn Concertos Numbers
  1 & 4, 65
Jupiter Symphony, 54
Kegelstatt Trio, 53
Linz Symphony, 117
logo, 98
The Magic Flute, 55
memorabilia (Apple Creek
  Flowers), 49
"Mozart as a Mason" talk, 54
Mozart Dances and Marches, 55
Oboe Concerto, 53, 103
Piano Concerto No. 7, 116
Piano Concerto No. 14, 55
Piano Quartet, K. 493, 55
Piano Quartet, K. 478, 116
Posthorn Serenade, 40
Sinfonia Concertante for Violin
  and Viola, 53, 97
Symphony No. 40, 43, 54, 121
Violin Concerto No. 3, 79
The Mozart Festival Society, 46, 53
Mullova, Viktoria, 41
"The Music Paradigm" leadership
  approaches, 122–123
Muspratt, Kirk, 38, 40

N

Naperville Sun, 22

National Keyboard Arts, 15–16

Neidich, Charles, 57–58, *60*

Nelson, Alexandra, 115

Nelson, Peter, 61–62

New York Times Arts and Leisure Summer Stages, 78

Nierenberg, Roger, "The Music Paradigm," leadership and, 122–123

O

Oktoberfest, 100

Ormrod, Richard, 53

Osadchy, Eugene, 61, 64, *65*

Ottens, Al, 99, 100, *111*, 125

Ottens, Amy, 99, 100, *111*

Owen, Blythe, 11

P

Pearce, Elvina, 15

Peck, Donald, 51, 61

Peck, Richard, 91

Pelligrini, Norm, 52

Pensinger, Lynn, 63–64, *112*

Pensinger, Ray, 33–34, 38, 41–42, *48*, 55, 59, 62–63, 68, *112*

Peskanov, Mark, 42–43, *47*, 51–53, 58–59, 64, *67*, *70*, 79, 96, 133

artistic director collaboration, 58–60

festival bio, 58–59

violinist and conductor, 53

Peters, Suzy, 92–94, 98

piano quartet, 9n

Piccirilli, Dolores, 17

Pipal, Erin, *110*

Place de la Musique, 113–117, 119

2015 benefit, 120–121

Gruppman, Igor and Vesna, *120*

Ponstein, Denise Graff, 91

Portnoy, Marsha, 40

Potter, Mike, x

Primakov, Vassily, 107, *107*

Prosseda, Roberto, 135

Pump House Flowers, 89

Q

quilt raffle, 100

R

Radwanska, Ewa, 94, 113, *113*

Ravinia Festival, 78

Rawlins, Dot, 92, *93*, 100

reverse fundraising, 32

Rile, Joanne, 79–80

RJ Recording and Sound, 91

Robbins, Gerald, 64

Rubinstein, Artur, 9, 127, 137

S

Salzbrunn, Steve, 90, 98

Sanfilippo, Marian and Jasper, 113

Sarasate
  "Ziguenerweisen", 71, 133
Scharres, John, *90*
Schiffer, Isabel, *100*
Schiffer, Mark, 39, 99, *100*
Schiszik, Brenda, 91
Schiszik, Jerry, 91
Schoonmaker, William, 13
Schrader, David, 36–37, 101, *101*, 119
Shupp, Erica, 121
Smith, Karen, 68
Sodini, Vivian B., 107, *110*
Sollak, Karl, 35, 36–37, 41, 51
Solti, George, 34
Solti, Valerie, 34
Sommerville, James, 64
spending issues, 124–125
Stage Left Cafe, 95
Steinway L purchase, 12
Steller, Joanne, 77
Stewart, Roberta, 92
Stokowski, Leopold, 2
Stork, Betty Thomas, 136
Stravinsky, Françoise, 115n
Stravinsky, Soulima, 13, 115n
Stravinsky Connection
  Cooper, Emil, 10
  Nelson, Alexandra and, 115
  Stravinsky, Soulima, 13
Streit, Ed, 66, 95, *99*

Stromberg, Allen, 82
Suk, Mykola, 96, 120
  and Igor Gruppman, 121
Sun City Huntley's Let's Dance Band, 119
Susan Peters Associates, 92–93
Svoboda, Sonia, *110*
Svoboda, Tom, *99,* 99–100
Swan, Jeffrey, 78–79, 95
Swisher, Martha, ix
Symphony Magazine, 105–106

T
Tchivzhel, Edvard, 38, 41–43, *47,* 51–52
Teaching Little Fingers to Play, 7
Thomas, Betty, 49
Thüringer Salonquintett, 62
TRG (Target Research Group Arts), 76–78
  analytics in marketing, 76–78
  new marketing techniques, 98

V
Vajda, Gregory, 134
Vakarelis, Janis, 51–52
Vienna Piano Trio, 134
Vinokur, Olga, 81
Vivaldi
  Four Seasons 95,117

W

Warner, Wendy, 82

Weinrod, Bill, 24

Wester, Elizabeth (Beth), 30–35, *36, 63, 83*

trophy for recognition, *83*

Wester, Jim, 63, *129*

WFMT, 98.7, 39, 52

Whalen, Anita, *23, 47, 48, 70, 84*

ballet lessons, 7–8

Baton Rouge, 8–9

birth announcement, *Orpheus in the Underworld,* 1

births of children, 15

Chopin, favorite composer at age 3, 2

cultural education from grandparents, 4

father's violin playing, 2–3

grandmother, 3–4

high school years, 11–13

marriage, 14

Met broadcasts on Saturdays, *La Bohème,* 5

move to Connecticut, 6

music class performance of "Happy Birthday," 6–7

music experiences, 10

music instruction

certification as instructor, 16–17

receiving in early life, 7–9

Offutt Air Force Base piano students, 14–15

piano lessons, 7

giving at Offutt Air Force Base, 14–15

reading music, 8–9

"Windy City Boogie," 9

Whalen, Charlie, *129*

legal matters for festival, 63

meeting, 14–15, 48–49

Whalen, Chuck, 15

"The Music Paradigm" leadership program, 122–123

Whalen, Julia, 15

Whitney, Charles, 61

Whitney, Joan, 61

Winter, Pat, 41–42

Wipfli LLP, 90

Woodfest, 29

Woodstock Mozart Festival, ix, 26–29, 39, 42, 59, 78, 123–125

1996 season, 51–52

1997 season, 53–54

1998 season, 54–56, 57–58

2000 season, 64

2002 season, 69–72, 74–76

2006 season, 78–81

2007 season, 81–84

2010 season, 89–90

2012 season, 105–112

artwork, 29–30

Chef's Showcase Brunch, 39
closing, 125–126
initial contact and hiring,
    26–28
recovery from previous deficit,
    31–34, 48
seventh season, 36
Symphony Magazine photo of
    banner, *106*
Woodstock Opera House, 26–30,
    50–51, 90, 116–117, 120
2015 benefit, 120–121
Conductor/Artist Conversa-
    tions, 51–52
notable alumni, 28
Scharres, John, *90*
Stage Left Cafe, 95

Z
Zanck, Charie, 46, *48*
Zanck, Tom, 46, *48*
Zell, Helen (Herzog), 9n

www.ingramcontent.com/pod-product-compliance
Lightning Source LLC
Chambersburg PA
CBHW051525120626

46551CB00012B/1086